W9-BSD-485

MoonPie

↓

MoonPie

BIOGRAPHY *of an*
Out-of-This-World
SNACK

↓

DAVID MAGEE

ISBN-10: 0-97189-748-4
ISBN-13: 978-0-97189-748-9
Library of Congress Catalog Card Number: 2006921092

MoonPie® is a registered trademark of Chattanooga Bakery, Inc.
Photos courtesy of Chattanooga Bakery, Inc.
Editing by Henry Oehmig
Book Design by Fiona Raven

First Printing September 2006
Printed in Canada

Published by Jefferson Press

j e f f e r s o n   p r e s s

P.O. Box 115
Lookout Mountain, TN 37350
www.jeffersonpress.com

For Kent Rasco Magee,
an out-of-this-world wife.

Contents

🡇

"We may not understand why we freak. We may have no conscious control over our allegiances. But they arise from our most sacred fears and desires and, as such, they represent the truest expression of our selves."

— Steve Almond, author, *Candyfreak*

More Than a Memory

↓

"The first breakfast I ever fixed for my husband, over 40 years ago, was a MoonPie and an R.C. Cola. We never eat a MoonPie now without recalling our first breakfast as husband and wife."

—Arcell Sawyer, Clayton, North Carolina

FOR THE LONGEST TIME, I thought my MoonPie attraction was merely the result of recollected fondness. That's what made the most sense anyway, considering that, as a young adult, I seldom foraged for snacks with the slightest hints of sweetness. Yes, I was among those youth who would devour the previous week's cold pizza at midmorning when the routine of two eggs or a cup of yogurt turned dull and tasteless; and then there were fried pork skins in the afternoon when the thought of a healthy sandwich or salad had all but evaporated. Yet munching on a candy bar at any time of the day as that old, familiar, stomach pang repeatedly punched my *EAT* button? This feeding impulse rarely happened with me—but when it did, there was just one item that could satisfy my moody, teenage appetite.

These occasions that called for a comforting snack always led me to a round, aptly named, somewhat-sweet food made of double layers of marshmallow and cookie, which were hidden beneath a chocolate, vanilla or banana coating. Nothing else would do. Not the dry-roasted, salted peanuts stacked to the left, not the red, toxic-looking Hot Fries chips shelved at the bottom. Claiming the center of my world in these dear moments was always a MoonPie, "The Original Marshmallow Sandwich." It washed down well with a soda, and each bite, as I recall, was savored and flavored by the touch of dread that every smacking mouthful only meant less of the snack remained. As much as I still enjoy taking down a MoonPie today, I admit that my mind tends to scroll back through the years and replay nostalgic clips of when I first felt the snack's influence—moments that, as Steve Almond explains, were critical to shaping my character and its lasting allegiances.

From its rather humble beginning in 1917 at Chattanooga Bakery, Inc., located in—you guessed it—Chattanooga, Tennessee, the MoonPie emerged during the middle part of the 20th century as a food staple for Southern snack seekers. By 1970, the year when I turned five and became mature enough to retain images of people and places, MoonPies were prominently featured in most every thriving, viable country store and market below the Mason-Dixon Line. So it was with great anticipation that, upon the twice-a-year visits to my grandfather's home in rural East Mississippi, I would accompany my grandfather on his daily trip to the store to get the mail.

He was a farmer in the days when a man having just one running tractor, less than 500 acres, and a willingness to work sunrise to sundown could earn enough money to own land, a house and his equipment outright. He also managed to save enough to send his daughter to college, and he had the change left over to buy his voracious grandson a small sack of treats each time he took me to the store with him. The mail, in that place, at that time, was not delivered box to box by a rural route carrier. Rather, residents of the area kept a post office box at the country store, which was served by a proprietor acting both as market manager and postmaster. The daily trip to the store for my grandfather could have just as easily yielded bags of sugar and flour as it could bills from the electric and gas companies. For me, though, it was all about getting the goodies.

Typically, it was summertime when I visited my grandfather's small house, set some two hundred yards off a clickity-clack blacktop road, and my daily routine was to wake up midmorning, search out a cartoon or game show on the lone, rabbit-eared, black-and-white television, which projected a fuzzy signal from just three stations, before wandering out to the yard just prior to noon where I poked and prodded the ground with a stick, listening for his old, blue pickup to make the shift from the road in front of the house to the gravel driveway. I remember it being hot while I waited for him outside. As the locusts whirred and the wasps droned beneath the eaves of the house, sweat would run down my nose and slide from underneath my arms to the crimped waistband of my shorts. But I didn't dare go inside for fear I would miss the drive that happened only once a weekday.

Without fail, my grandfather would pull into the gravel driveway a few minutes before noon, come to a stop, and push open the squeaky passenger door. I climbed aboard, gathering his smell of a morning's work and taking note of the weathered nape of his neck, which was so wrinkled and divided by deep troughs that it looked more like the map of the states I had played with in preschool than actual skin.

The store was less than a mile down the blacktop road, which was fortunate considering any longer of a drive would have been torture. The building didn't look like much. It was built from unpainted and worn clapboard, and faded Coca-Cola and R.C. Cola signs decorated the front door. There was a single gas pump in front that still operated but had to be hand-primed first. And the boards of the porch which led to the entrance had partially sunk into the ground, creating a semi-earth, semi-floor illusion.

Inside the store, however, beauty abounded. Mostly, this came in the form of colorful wrappers and boxes holding more snack and candy items than a young mind could grasp. There were Now & Later's, Goo Goo Clusters, and a vast assortment of Double Bubble flavors. And there were MoonPies. Lots of MoonPies. All Single Decker and mostly chocolate, the MoonPies were sold from open cartons situated prominently on the right side of the cash register.

Here lay youthful nirvana in all its multi-colored and sugar-saturated forms.

My routine was to head straight to the register where long, skinny sacks were stacked, and I would fill my bag with candy and treats, particularly gum and other sour, chewy things. Once the bag held all that I could respectfully ask my grandfather to buy, I returned to the counter to choose a MoonPie. It wouldn't fit into the narrow sack, but that didn't matter. Before we had even turned back into the gravel driveway on our way home, I would be shaking the last chocolate crumbs from the MoonPie wrapper into my mouth.

Then, a couple of short years after these first MoonPie recollections took place, my grandfather passed away. For a time following his death, I lost interest in the round, delectable treats. I'm sure I ate one here and there, but roughly seven years would pass before I fell back into the old, blissful habit of binging on MoonPies for days in a row. And this time it wasn't a family member who sparked the old magic, but a friend.

A boy named Biff was the imaginative leader of our Oxford, Mississippi, summertime bunch of friends that, being in our final year before adolescence, obsessed over baseball and homeruns instead of girls. Every day we gathered in our neighbor's sprawling backyard, perfectly encased by a chain-link fence, and played homerun derby for hours on end. When we got too hungry to go another inning, we scattered to various homes to refuel.

But on one particular day, Biff recalled seeing his mother charge groceries at a small, family-owned market just down the street. It was so simple, he explained to us. All she did was gather items, ask a man to charge them, sign a tiny slip of paper and—*presto!*—she could take the goods home. Not one to let such opportunity slip away, Biff invited the gang to follow him to the market, where he pledged to buy snacks and candy for all. Having no money and fearing the offer too good to be true, I arrived at the checkout counter with only a carton of fruit punch. Biff looked insulted.

"That isn't enough," he said. "Here."

He tossed on the counter before me a chocolate MoonPie and reached into an adjacent box and grabbed a banana one for himself. As I sat outside on the searing curb, eating my MoonPie, I couldn't help but think of the country store and my grandfather's old, blue truck and the wrinkled nape of his neck.

Biff took us back to the store for many successive days, which seemed to span an entire month, and each time I got another MoonPie, inspiring and bringing back more fond memories. But then the calendar changed as one month gave way to another, and Biff abruptly quit taking us to the store for free snacks. In hindsight, I'm sure this coincided with the day that his parents finally got the bill, but all we knew was that after one grueling game in early August, Biff called the group to a halt as we instinctively began walking to the store.

"Let's just go to David's house," was all he said.

For the next two decades, the MoonPie would pop into my daily diet on occasion, and the thought of it came and went, like a favorite, out-of-town uncle; if I spotted the unmistakable snack at a grocery or convenience store, I immediately bought one, and we bonded like old times; but if our paths hadn't crossed for a while, the MoonPie kept a place in my mind with other pleasant memories. Then, as my own children grew old enough to form recollections of their own, the beloved snack reemerged. My oldest son, for instance, went away to summer camp for one month and returned with a strong affinity for banana-flavored, Double Decker MoonPies. Apparently, the boys gathered each Sunday night at the camp director's house, and the delicious lunar treats were passed out to all the campers with cold glasses of milk. It was not long before I converted to the banana flavor, too, and together we ate them, making for new, pleasant moments for both of us.

When my family moved in 2003 from northern Mississippi to the hills of East Tennessee—specifically, to the small town of Lookout Mountain, which rises to 1,950 feet, overlooking the city of Chattanooga—I made the acquaintance of the Sam Campbell III family, who, I was pleased to learn, own Chattanooga Bakery and its famous MoonPie brand. Curiously, I never broached the subject of the snack during friendly conversations with various members of the clan, perhaps because the snack was so close and personal after a nearly lifelong relationship.

However, as I worked for several years on books about such iconic American brands as Ford Motor Company and John Deere, I was struck by the ever-increasing idea that only a writer would know how to explore the intricacies of the quirky MoonPie. I was further intrigued when I learned that Chattanooga Bakery only made one product, just as I was flabbergasted by the number of people I encountered in person through my initial research, who shared similar stories of the MoonPie serving as a endearing connection to their past.

For instance, Patricia Marshall, an endearing woman now living in Texas, said her favorite childhood memory is riding in the car with her father as he delivered mail in the 1950s in rural Mississippi. Many residents, she told me, would wait by their mail box for them to come along. She was young and hopeful and remembers seeing not poverty, but a "proud and unique people who appreciated Daddy's smile and kind words."

"It was our tradition to stop along the way at a little country store for MoonPies warmed by summer breezes," she said. "These days I warm the MoonPies in the microwave, but they are still my ultimate comfort food, reminding me of my daddy, happy times and smiling faces."

Another woman, Martha Deming Gray of Jackson, Tennessee, has vivid MoonPie memories dating back more than sixty years. She can recall a time when she and her two sisters, Oneida and Willie Sue, lived in the small West Tennessee town of Silverton as young girls. They were allowed to leave the schoolhouse during the lunch hour to run home to check for eggs laid by the family's hens. The girls would gather the eggs and take them to a nearby country store, trading them for MoonPies and Pepsi Colas. Often, she said, classmates Curtis Fry and Buster Murley, would be there eating MoonPies and drinking Pepsi Colas as well. Her sister, Willie Sue, was so affected by this experience that during the 1941–1942 school year she wrote a poem about it.

MoonPies

Buster Murley again once more
Will eat his dinner at Raymond Fitts' Store
And with his boyfriend Curtis Fry
They will buy a Pepsi Cola and MoonPie.

To Curtis the Pepsi Cola and MoonPie is a Grand Old Dinner
But the MoonPies are making him thinner and thinner.
To Buster the MoonPie hits the spot. Two big bites, that's a lot
And on a Pepsi Cola he can sip
But the MoonPies are putting his butt in the eclipse.

The more I learned about the MoonPie, the more I wanted to rekindle my long-running relationship. It only made sense considering Chattanooga Bakery was huffing and puffing out thousands upon thousands of the marshmallow sandwiches each day in my midst. With its headquarters located near the winding Tennessee River in downtown Chattanooga, I imagined the smell of warm chocolate and marshmallow and cookie wafting miles from the plant, scaling up the steep but unimposing cliffs of Lookout Mountain, and softly reaching my nose. In response, I asked my wife one day to so kindly bring home a MoonPie from a shopping excursion. "No," I said, changing my mind, "make that a carton of MoonPies, please." To my delight, she obliged, though when she returned, it was with something unfamiliar. A MoonPie, yes, but not in the tradition recalled through so many memories. While the snacks looked the same, smelled the same, and tasted the same, one attribute was obviously different— the size. These MoonPies were smaller—a mini version, as the label read. The original Single Decker was still around, my wife informed me, as was the ever-popular Double Decker.

As it turned out, the Mini MoonPie was merely a contemporary variation of this decades-old brand, a new spin on time-tested goodness.

Without hesitation, I ate one of the banana-coated Mini MoonPies, then another, and another. In less than two days, the box of minis was gone. I asked for, and received, another box, which quickly found the same demise. My idea was that through immersion, I would better understand the complexities that blend together to create such a rich, palatable experience. Soon, however, I came to understand I was developing a full-fledged addiction. I tried to cut down to one mini a day but found this difficult. I thought, perhaps, that a worthy and profitable invention might be some sort of MoonPie patch, one that oozed flavor into my veins to alleviate the cravings, and it did not have to be banana, either. Any of the three would do. The feeling was so strong, I found myself coming up with internal, lyrical demands:

Banana MoonPie,
Chocolate MoonPie,
Vanilla MoonPie,

I need a MoonPie,
Or baby won't you patch me up?

But I began to realize that the experience for me, as well as for generations of others, was just as much about memories as it was the flavor which triggered them. So, I turned my intrigue into a personal mission. My idea was to learn how a food product so simple and of-the-moment can at the same time be so seductive and long-lasting. I called on Sam Campbell IV, my down-the-street neighbor who serves as president of Chattanooga Bakery, and announced my intention of doing the unusual: researching and writing the biography of a snack. I was afraid he might roll his eyes or, worse yet, stop waving to me when we drove past each other in the neighborhood or met at one of the four-way stops.

"To what level you have stooped?" I imagined him asking me. "Two years ago you were chronicling the life and times of Henry Ford's great-grandson. Now you want to write a biography of the MoonPie?"

I had also prepared my honest, straightforward response: "I can't help it."

Fortunately, I did not need the latter explanation, since something Campbell and his family have obviously learned in their years of stewardship and guidance is that the iconic product has for more than eighty years lived a life of its own, weaving together a cultural fabric of time and place marked by flavor that so many of us are a part of.

"Well," he said, "I'm not sure you will find all you need for a whole book, but I suppose if any snack deserves a biography it's the MoonPie, just because it's so much bigger than us all."

Sitting with Campbell in his offices at Chattanooga Bakery and attempting to turn back the hands of time and trace the steps of the MoonPie from the beginning, it seemed important before jumping into the tall-but-true and exceptionally sweet tale to put the snack's eminence into proper perspective. Without addressing this properly, I thought it might be difficult for some to appreciate the small and subtle steps taken by the MoonPie during its decades-long journey.

I knew it would prove difficult—or even impossible—to find a way to successfully state the scope of the MoonPie in just a few short words. But as Campbell sat across the table, sharing reflections on the snack with an easy smile and kind words, and avoided effusive praise for the treat like a proud father trying not to brag on his children, I wondered if the snack's most telling and impacting epithet might not be told in words but simply in numbers. After all, people find intrigue in the bold statement made by America's most recognized fast-food chain, which has served "billions" of hamburgers through the years. So why not do a little math and calculate the total production of America's original marshmallow sandwich?

"Do you have any idea how many MoonPies have been produced through the years?" I asked.

If anyone knew the answer, it would be Campbell. The third-generation leader of the family company, proclaimed by one leading financial source as a "MoonPie magnate," has been at the helm since the late 1980s and as an avid student of business and history, he has pored over the company's own internal financials and production documents dating back decades. Surprisingly, he did not have the instant answer to my question, but the interrogation did strike curiosity. Quickly putting a pencil to paper, Campbell began to calculate for what must have been five minutes or more. The last fifteen years or so were easy, he said, multiplying the one million pies made each business day when baking lines are up and running at full capacity. For the production of previous years, he made educated assumptions in round numbers decade-by-decade, based on general period production trends in the company's history.

"Hmmm," he said, looking up from the figure. "That's a lot of MoonPies."

"How many?"

"It looks like four billion," Campbell said, smiling shyly,

before looking back down to double check the math. "I know it is right, probably even more, but that just sounds like a lot. Let's just say three billion."

Yes, I told him, but consider how long the MoonPie has been around and all the people who have consumed them through the years. I had five last week and probably more the week before. And, that does not compare to all those I devoured under the guidance of my grandfather, or later with my friend Biff. I'm a freak, I know, but I'm not the only one. What about the rumor I heard concerning O.J. Simpson? Apparently, when O.J. was in detention during trial, sales of banana-flavored MoonPies by one California distributor soared. I guess "The Juice" needed a patch as well, and his affinity for the flavor spread to others in detention like a wildfire fueled by strong winds, creating unusual demand from an unsuspecting area. And think about how many other freaks, like Curtis Fry and Buster Murley, have consumed MoonPies since the snack's inception. Those of us belonging to this passionate minority can easily lay claim to a billion pies, if not more.

We need to go public with this, I told Campbell. The MoonPie nation, which has engulfed these snacks one memory-forming bite at a time, must know what it has accomplished. Nothing else would crystallize the importance of this snack for people like that significant, head-turning number. If it is okay for McDonald's to advertise "billions served," we can at least be forthcoming and place the illustrious marshmallow sandwich on its rightful perch. So, I asked once again, seeking an official, on-the-record response that would, in just a few short words, set the tone for a thorough exploration of a brand that seems so simple but, in reality, is not.

"Okay," Campbell said. "Since the beginning, we've produced three-to-four billion MoonPies."

And so begins the story of an out-of-this-world snack . . .

A Portable Snack

↓

"I grew up in Harlan, Kentucky, the city where 'Coal is king, and guests are royalty.' In the summer I spent most of my time in Kitts, Kentucky, visiting my grandparents. My grandfather was an electrician in the Kitts mines, and the center of the community was the company store, the commissary. I could spend a nickel a day and put it on the tab. I always went for the MoonPie. The ritual was to spin it around once, look up at the sky and drop that last bite into my mouth. I got to lick the rest of the chocolate off my hands on the walk home."

—Tish P., Lexington, Kentucky

WHEN CHATTANOOGA BAKERY began operation in Chattanooga, Tennessee, in the early 1900s, it was little more than a small offshoot of the prominent Mountain City Flour Mill, owned by the Hutcheson family. At the time, the mill decided to create this spin-off business in order for the new bakery to use leftover flour that was unsalable to the public. When wheat was milled in those days, many different grades of flour were left over from the final, premium flour product, some of which were useable in baked goods. Through the creation of a bakery, what was previous flour waste from the mill became a major ingredient in its small, subsidiary business. No sense wasting good, available flour.

Run by mill employee John Campbell, the bakery began producing items like ginger snaps since, if enough ginger was added to the leftover flour, "they became good." Other popular Chattanooga Bakery items included vanilla wafers, lemon cookies, and fig bars. Those that were not private label items were billed under the bakery's Lookout brand, a trade name derived from the bakery's King Street location in the industrialized section of Chattanooga, which had a clear view of

Lookout Mountain's rising prominence, the geographic icon which elevates to a dramatic point some 2,000 feet above the Tennessee Valley. Among the hundred or more products marketed by the bakery under the Lookout brand were Lookout Raisin Cookies, Lookout Sugar Cookies, and the Lookout Salty Cracker. But the marshmallow sandwich now known as the MoonPie was not in production, as it had not yet been invented.

However, by 1910 Chattanooga Bakery was making more than two hundred other items in all, and while the business was considerably smaller in size than the flourishing Mountain City Flour Mill, it was a growing, viable operation in Chattanooga, a city known at the time as "the Pittsburgh of the South" that was situated along the banks of the Tennessee River and had a major presence in iron manufacturing. It was an industrial area for the most part that also, ironically, had a handful of budding entrepreneurs focused on consumer brand products.

It was in Chattanooga, for instance, that a popular fountain drink named Coca-Cola was brought to consumers en masse in large part due to the vision of three pioneer lawyers, who, after gaining bottling rights to Coca-Cola in 1899 for the grand sum of $1, granted rights to so many territorial bottlers that by 1909 there were more than four hundred in America. Another consumer product enterprise, Chattanooga Medicine Company, was founded in the city in the late 1800s. Now operating as Chattem, the manufacturer of items like Gold Bond and Bull Frog Sunblock got its start selling the once-popular Theodore's Black Draught, a senna-based laxative that was popular in the United States and Britain in the first half of 20th century.

Chattanooga Bakery, however, was not growing at nearly the same pace of Coca-Cola Bottling, or Chattanooga Medicine Company for that matter, largely because of fierce competition in baked goods throughout the southern region it served. It was a sign of the times in which the production and sale of baked goods was highly regionalized, if not local- ized, throughout the country; difficulties existed in shipping product long distances because of undeveloped roads and the simplicity of first-generation automobiles. As a result, many of Chattanooga Bakery's private label products were more commodities than specialties in the ultra-competitive marketplace, and with each year following the company's product-mix peak in 1910, unprofitable items were dropped from the lineup.

At some time during or around 1917, the MoonPie was created, but it was hardly met with any fanfare or buzz at Chattanooga Bakery. Actually, many of the precise details of its creation have remained a bit of a mystery, even to those closely associated with the bakery. For the longest time, nobody was exactly sure how the original marshmallow sandwich came to be; there were merely broad facts involving a company sales-man, coal miners and sales of a marshmallow sandwich snack, which began showing up on old company records. Not real-izing what a non-event the creation of the first MoonPie had been, I expected, when first asking Campbell about the birth of the snack, to be led to a company vault containing archives and memorabilia, including the first advertisements for the MoonPie and records of internal communications document-ing the thought processes behind its creation.

But Campbell quickly let me know their records show the introduction of the MoonPie was no big deal at the company since it was merely the addition of yet another baked good to an already deep lineup. Even after many private label foods had been dropped from production, Chattanooga Bakery was still making dozens and dozens of items, from lemon cookies to ginger snaps, so the addition of one more was not necessarily a heralded event. And there is no evidence the creation of the MoonPie was considered revolutionary or head-turning to the snack-consuming public. To the contrary, its advent was undoubtedly a moment of very little significance—seemingly another bakery selection offered in a crowded marketplace.

Short of any actual records or documentation, lore purports that at some point before the Moonpie was created by the bakery, a general manager who worked for Mountain City Flour Mill was out selling in the field, seeking orders for bakery goods. During a stop in the coal-mining, Appalachian region of Kentucky, the general manager became frustrated when no orders were placed for the snack foods he was trying to sell.

"They don't want anything we have," he supposedly reported to Chattanooga.

For decades, nobody was exactly sure where the salesman was at the time nor what name he went by, though it was thought to be Earl Mitchell. This was only educated lore, however, since there are no pictures in existence of Mitchell with a MoonPie, just as there are no records from those days linking him to the snack's creation. But the mystery was somewhat solved in the mid-1980s when a humorous, paperback book written by Ron Dickson was released in 1985 by Peachtree Publishers. A compilation of wit related to "the world's greatest snack," *The Great American MoonPie HandBook* is a mixture of satire and fact, which pays homage to the original marshmallow sandwich.

As the self-professed leader and lifelong president of the MoonPie Cultural Club, Dickson made tongue-in-cheek suggestions in his book such as how the "marshmallow from a MoonPie can be used to make a temporary patch in an inner tube" for a bicycle tire; that "the frozen chocolate Double Decker MoonPie makes an excellent hockey puck;" and that nothing will make mother happier on her special day than the gift of a case of MoonPies. Also in the lighthearted book, Dickson gives advice on "how to raise children by bribing them with MoonPies" and how the MoonPie can be made a "wonderful accessory to love."

The book's release sparked stories about the snack in several leading newspapers, including *The New York Times*, in which the writer noted, "The name of the visionary has been lost in the fog of history." In another newspaper article, one journalist mused that "like Stonehenge, MoonPies carry an air of mystery and a cozy sense of permanence." The article's author was particularly impressed with the fact that the creation of the MoonPie remained in question, suggesting in the lead that "like all good legends, the origin of the Moon Pie is shrouded in mystery."

But as fortune would have it, the mystery would not remain shrouded for long since the story was reprinted in the Charlotte, North Carolina newspaper, and one noteworthy reader found it interesting that nobody seemed to be positively sure that a man named Earl Mitchell came up with the idea for the first MoonPie. The reader's name: Earl Mitchell Jr. He promptly contacted the book's author, Dickson, as well as then-MoonPie Vice President John Kosik, telling them he was sure it was his father, since deceased, who was responsible for the creation of the MoonPie.

"My daddy was the Knoxville branch manager of the Mountain City Flour Mill," said Earl Mitchell Jr. at the time. "Everybody knows Daddy invented the MoonPie."

He told Dickson and Kosik stories of riding as a young man with his father as he called on clients in southeastern Kentucky and Tennessee, selling items for Chattanooga Bakery and Mountain City Flour Mill. It was on these sales road trips that Earl Mitchell Jr. said his father explained to him the details of the MoonPie's origin. The story goes that his father was making a sales call to a store in a Kentucky coal mining region that catered heavily to miners. These were men who worked all day long in soot-soaked underground shafts, chiseling the coal into chunks and loading them into waiting carts, which were whisked away one after another in an endless, monotonous ritual. When the break whistle blew, these mining men wanted a hearty snack, not a small package of lemon cookies or ginger snaps.

Mitchell was surprised and reportedly dismayed to learn none of the Chattanooga Bakery products were wanted for stocking by the commissary manager. Not willing to take no for an answer, Mitchell is said to have walked up to a group of miners on break, asking them what type of snack they wanted, since there was no interest in the company's standard fare. In response, one miner stood up and held his hands together, declaring they wanted something large and filling for lunch pails.

"About that big," the miner said, his hands framed in the shape of the moon, pointing toward the sky.

At this point, Mitchell could have taken the miner's recommendation and responded in a number of ways that might have been fatal to the conception of the original marshmallow sandwich. He could have seen a giant version of Lookout Lemon Biscuit as the perfect solution to the miner's request, or stacking a couple of Lookout Honey Cakes on top of a pat of peanut butter. We freaks can be thankful that Mitchell took a different direction in his snack-seeking quest.

Upon returning to Chattanooga Bakery and Mountain City Flour Mill, the salesman reportedly noticed company workers dipping freshly made graham cookies, one of the bakery's leading production items, into vats of freshly made marshmallow, then laying them in a windowsill at the plant to dry and harden before eating. The sight was apparently an epiphany of sorts for Mitchell, the kind of moment which has occurred repeatedly in our national history where someone unknowingly alters the future of people, place and time, like Thomas Edison's invention of the light bulb or the first person to drop a slab of bologna in a frying pan.

Mitchell's idea was to stack one graham cookie on top of another, sandwich marshmallow in between, and top the concoction with a thick layer of creamy chocolate. The result was a snack that was large, filling, in the shape of the moon, and sweet and tasteful—just what the miner ordered. Mitchell then took samples of the original marshmallow sandwich back to the store in the mining town, getting a positive response on the spot, understandably. Recognizing sales potential, other salesmen of Mountain City Flour Mill and Chattanooga Bakery took the marshmallow sandwich into the field, finding similar positive responses from consumers and store owners. Soon, Chattanooga Bakery was filling orders for the Lookout MoonPie.

For the price of a nickel, consumers got a snack that was more than four full inches round in diameter, filled with marshmallow, encased by two cookies, and coated in a thick layer of chocolate. One can only imagine the expressions of miners who tasted and experienced the first MoonPies. Accustomed to smaller-sized and less creative snacks like shortbread cookies and cakes, they probably could not believe the soft, gooey, cookie treat, with a coating that on hot days might have left a little chocolate around the corners of mouths to match the color of coal-dust residue on faces, and only cost five cents.

The freak was on.

"It was a big seller in the coal fields where [the workers] did not make much money," Earl Mitchell Jr. recalled. "They were getting a great big pie for a nickel. It would help them get to the next meal."

The emergence of Earl Mitchell Jr. and the confirmation of his father's role in the invention of the MoonPie led to another newspaper story when the Charlotte newspaper, upon learning of the new information about the MoonPie invention, sent a reporter to get the scoop, announcing the news under the headline: "Creator of the MoonPie Rediscovered." Years later, the man said to have had the idea for the first MoonPie was honored in memoriam by his granddaughter, Anna Pratt, who marked his grave site with a new marker on his North Carolina resting place. It reads: *Earl W. Mitchell, inventor of the legendary Southern snack, MoonPie, 1917.*

"I'm sorry Dad did not patent that thing," joked Earl Mitchell Jr. "Man, I would have a Cadillac on each foot now."

Even though the MoonPie apparently launched from Chattanooga Bakery with little fanfare, the snack found quick popularity in the southeastern region primarily served by the Southeast Tennessee company. The Lookout MoonPie quickly became a top-selling product in North Carolina and in the hills of Kentucky and eastern Tennessee, the Appalachian regions which suffered from poverty and prized the large size and small price of the MoonPie. Increasingly, the original marshmallow sandwich became a volume leader for Chattanooga Bakery; and others items, like many of the company's private label snacks, were dropped year after year as they proved to be less profitable due to strong competition for common items.

After all, the MoonPie in its flavorful and satiating glory was a signature product, and a soda cracker was a soda cracker, such staples being produced by most every bakery operating in the South. Therefore, with each passing day of business, the snack as big as the moon that was birthed by a salesman trying to meet the hunger pangs of a miner was fast growing in stature as a tasty treat.

John Campbell continued running Chattanooga Bakery through its growth phase, and with the company showing promise, strengthened by the increasingly popular Lookout MoonPie, he needed help. So in the afternoons his entrepreneurial, management-minded brother, Sam H. Campbell Jr.

came into the office to assist with duties. An oil distributor running Campbell Oil Company and several other businesses, including radio stations, Sam H. Campbell Jr. faced a difficult choice when his brother, John, died suddenly in 1938. Chattanooga Bakery seemed the least attractive of all his diversified businesses interests, but for some reason, the bakery interested Sam H. Campbell Jr. enough that he never considered selling it upon his brother's death.

Instead, he kept his routine of working at the oil company in the mornings and overseeing the bakery in the afternoons. Shortly thereafter, he purchased the bakery outright along with a partner, Bobby Jones, so that the company was no longer a subsidiary of Mountain City Flour Mill. The mill, incidentally, was sold by the Hutcheson family to a Memphis firm in the 1940s. Over the next several years, Sam H. Campbell Jr. sold interests in most of his other businesses, concentrating almost exclusively on the bakery even though it was "not a terrifically prosperous business" in comparison to his previous enterprises.

"I've never really understood why he kept the bakery over

the others, but thank goodness he did," said Sam Campbell III, who took over leadership of the business upon his father's death in the 1950s and continued the family legacy of ownership and leadership until his oldest son, Sam Campbell IV, would manage it in the 1980s.

By the early 1940s, MoonPie production had steadily increased in volume while the production of other bakery items decreased to the point that only four or five other items, like the ginger snap and lemon cookie staples, remained in the lineup. But it was the MoonPie which was emerging as a shining star. The product surged rapidly in popularity from the Carolinas to Georgia to Tennessee because "it was a portable lunch—the original snack cake," and because the soft treat remained fresh for weeks after it was made and shipped to stores. This was a huge distinction from other traditional bakery goods at that time which often became stale in mere days. Together, such unique qualities made the original marshmallow sandwich a big hit with Southern consumers.

"The shelf life was long," says Sam Campbell III, "and

it was big and sweet and soft. In the Southeast and the Southwest (United States) soft was and is very important. In England, soft to them means the product is stale. Also, the graham cracker and the MoonPie were first cousins, and since the graham cracker was considered good for children, the MoonPie emerged as more of a treatment than a treat."

Working men could immediately make the items stocking a rather lonely lunch pale more appetizing with the addition of a MoonPie, and they could stay full between meals with heartiness and flavor for just a nickel. Also, children wanting a snack enjoyed the MoonPie's sweetness, while parents appreciated the value, as well as the more nutritious benefits of the treat's cookies and marshmallow compared to candy. It was then, as it is now, filling, and also satisfying and indulgent but not excessive.

Like most good things of the time which suffered interruption with the beginning of World War II, the MoonPie saw its ascent level off with the patriotic call of duty. An integral provider for the U.S. Army of medicines and packages, Chattanooga Medicine Company, now Chattem, was charged by the government as a leading provider of food and medicine packages sent to soldiers overseas. Included in the packages were "medicine biscuits" made by Chattanooga Bakery.

Ultimately, however, the changes in production would prove fortuitous and be the most defining moment for the MoonPie since its creation. In concentrating on the wartime needs, and due to a lack of supplies necessary to make other items, the bakery all but ceased production of its wide array of products. The company began concentrating solely on the MoonPie and medicine biscuits ordered by the military. When World War II ended, the hundreds of products once distributed by Chattanooga Bakery were just a memory, and the company's efforts, for the most part, centered on the lovable, round original marshmallow sandwich.

Made and sold under the Lookout brand name and sold to other regional bakeries as a private label item, the marshmallow sandwich resumed its quick rise to popularity after the war in the mostly rural southern region of the United States because of its value and unique flavor combination. Still costing just a nickel, the snack was recognized by many consumers as the most and the best they could get for their hard-to-come-by money. Or, in other words, people at the time who had an extra five cents and a hearty appetite often found that a MoonPie hit just the right spot.

It was during this period that the snack became linked with another Southern favorite, the soft drink R.C. Cola. Produced by the Royal Crown Company of Columbus, Georgia, beginning in 1934, the sweet cola was sold in bottles containing a full sixteen ounces of beverage—four more than competitors like Coca Cola—for the price of a nickel. The truth is, research reveals that Southerners were just as likely to pair a MoonPie with other regional favorite beverages like Barq's Root Beer or Nehi soda, but it is the RC Cola which became linked with the original marshmallow sandwich through both lore and recollection.

"My mother has always told me the reason I like MoonPies so much is because she walked two miles to the store every day to get a MoonPie and RC Cola while she was pregnant with me. I'm glad she did."

—Gwen S., Hopkins, South Carolina

So synonymous are RC Cola and MoonPie that the reasonable assumption made by most is that the companies worked hard to build co-existing brands. However, nothing could be farther from the truth since neither company made any effort to link the products. Instead, Southerners migrated to both after the Great Depression and the war because money was so tight among the largely rural population. The RC Cola cost a nickel, and the MoonPie cost a nickel, meaning that anyone with a dime could get full and satisfied. As a result, the combination of a MoonPie and an RC Cola became a sort of "instant fast food" lunch and combination snack in the South during the 1950s.

"They would buy Moonpies and RC Colas from the store because the MoonPie was the biggest snack cake they could get, and the RC Cola was the biggest drink they could get, and each was just a nickel," says John Campbell II, vice president of Chattanooga Bakery. "So they could get the whole thing for a dime . . . the working man's lunch."

As the snack and drink pairing grew in popularity, it was more than working men washing down MoonPies with

RC Cola. Chattanooga resident Laura Pittman's great uncle was a dentist who apparently believed good hygiene involved the consumption of treats. "He had a very interesting office," she recalled, "but every time you went, before you had your teeth cleaned, you had to drink an RC Cola and eat a MoonPie, then you got your teeth cleaned."

Strengthened by a hit country song released by Big Bill Lister in 1951 titled "Gimme an RC Cola and a MoonPie," the two products became irrevocably linked by Southern consumers in a memorable association that lives on in the minds of many today despite the fact that the co-branding occurred by pure happenstance. For instance, broach the subject of MoonPies with a lifelong resident of the South, and he or she is likely to respond with memories of RC Cola, even though the drink this person consumed along with their first original marshmallow sandwich would just as likely have been a Coca Cola or cold glass of milk.

What beverage MoonPies were most frequently associated with or chased with, be it RC Cola, grape soda or Coca Cola, is of little consequence, of course. All one needs to know about the original marshmallow sandwich in the 1950s is that it soared in popularity to the point that Chattanooga Bakery no longer had the resources to make anything else. To meet surging demand, it was all MoonPies, all the time.

Double Decker is Born

↓

"*My favorite MoonPie memory is from when I was expecting my first child. I seemed to crave the chocolate Double Decker MoonPie, and one night I got up in the middle of the night to sneak one while my husband was sleeping. I was too sleepy to sit up and eat it and fell asleep. The next morning my husband woke me up asking how the MoonPie got stuck on his t-shirt. Half asleep, I said I didn't know. Then he asked how all the crumbs got in the bed. We have laughed about this for a long time.*"

—Rebecca J., Stone Mountain, Georgia

WITH ITS MARSHMALLOW FILLING smashed between two unique-recipe cookies and all covered in flavored topping, the MoonPie from its very beginning has been driven to success by distinctive qualities that tickle the palate and satisfy desires of want. Though there have been other snacks made through the years which were good, most of these can no longer be found, meaning that good alone is not enough to survive. Take, for instance, the Marathon Bar, an eight-inch long chunk of braided caramel covered in chocolate; the candy was introduced by Mars, Inc. in 1973. A one-time personal favorite of mine because of its twisted shape, the bar had a legion of other loyal followers, but sales never grew much beyond average numbers, and Mars pulled the candy bar off the shelves by 1981.

For the Marathon Bar, flavor alone was not enough. Competing against Snickers, another bar produced by Mars, and the likes of Butterfinger and Heath, the Marathon Bar, however tasty and unique in design, never developed a growing fan base. On the other hand, the MoonPie had advantages outside of taste that began to parlay into significant growth in consumer consumption beginning in the mid-to-late 1950s.

Under the direction of Sam Campbell III—who had filled the company's leadership role as a young man after his father, Sam Campbell Jr., died of a heart attack and after Bobby Jones, the interim chief executive officer, died suddenly in an automobile accident—the bakery took advantage of improved transportation in the rural South to deliver more pies to more people in more places.

Thanks to new state and federal highways that began to spread in web-like fashion between the more populated areas in the South; and more road-worthy vehicles; and a sharp increase in the number of gasoline filling stations found along rural roads, transportation improvements in the 1950s served as a boundary-breaker for the MoonPie. Previously confined largely to states bordering Tennessee, like North Carolina, Kentucky, and Georgia, the enhanced mobility served as a sort of product slingshot, hurling marshmallow sandwiches from the bakery's production facility on King Street in downtown Chattanooga to open mouths of receptive, if not demanding, customers from Texas to Louisiana to Florida to Missouri. It was still mostly a Southern thing, with the bulk of sales taking place below the Mason-Dixon Line, but the big and soft snack was launched by unprecedented reception farther and farther from its home, becoming a true national product.

Chattanooga Bakery achieved this growth—putting nickel-priced MoonPies in the hands of hundreds of thousands more customers in most parts of the country—through a rather unconventional distribution system; there were no trucks adorned on the sides with images of the snack running to stores in towns like Tupelo, Mississippi, and Asheville, North Carolina. I had never really thought about it before, but upon investigation I was not surprised to learn that the bakery never ran its own trucks, since in all my days of traveling to towns across the South, I cannot recall a single image of a Chattanooga Bakery truck parked in front of a market, back open, with a route salesman removing stacks of product. I remember, of course, seeing trucks bearing logos from other popular Southern brands like Coca-Cola, RC Cola, and Toms brand snack foods, yet no Chattanooga Bakery trucks. MoonPies were delivered to market primarily by other bakeries, those already servicing stores with products from loaf bread to snack cakes.

This approach may seem strange at first, if not counter-productive, but Chattanooga Bakery's distribution arrangement worked exceptionally well for both the company and its many regional partners. In the beginning, these relationships formed because the company had many private label items that were re-branded and sold regionally by other bakeries, making the Chattanooga firm a "baker's baker." Over time, as the MoonPie increasingly became Chattanooga Bakery's primary product, the partnerships continued to work well since the marshmallow sandwich was a unique and, therefore, non-competitive product, serving more as an offering enhancement for the other bakeries, which acted as a middle man. Most baking companies made their own ginger snaps and lemon cookies and various other snack cakes, but none had the original marshmallow sandwich.

Chattanooga Bakery produced the MoonPies, and shipped them to wholesale bakery partners across the country, which then sold the product to convenience stores and markets in their own service area. Typically, the regional bakeries had close-knit relationships with the retail store owners, and since they were already making calls to sell and stock their own products, the MoonPie fit in as a complement and sales advantage. As a result, the other bakeries not only sold and stocked the MoonPie, they actively promoted it.

"The product fit better with bakeries," said Sam Campbell III. "It was positioned as a long-shelf-life cake because of its size and price, and the shelf life was twice as long as the other products they were selling. Also, it was more marshmallow than cookie, meaning it did not compete directly with most other items."

The primary market for the MoonPie in this era was single-unit sales in food markets and rural stores, but in the late 1950s, the product found a home outside of the South for the first time due to one of history's greatest migrations, the two-decade period in which millions of black Americans moved north from the South in search of opportunity in both jobs and living environment. Finding work in industrialized cities like Chicago, Illinois, and Detroit, Michigan, hundreds of thousands of Southerners moved north in the movement that began in the late 1930s and continued for a quarter of a century: black migrant workers leaving low-paying, sun-baked jobs on hardscrabble Southern farms for better pay and a better quality of life, which resulted from burgeoning industries like the automotive.

Similar to the European immigrants who brought their favorite customs, such as tea, to the United States, or the immigrants who, crossing the border from Mexico to the United States in search of better jobs, carry with them cultural aspects and items like corn meal tortillas, these migrant workers from the South took their preferred tastes to the Motor and Windy cities. It was as if they moved north but never left the South behind, which was good news for a beloved snack like the MoonPie.

It only makes sense. I mean, leaving life on the Southern farm in the days before widespread rural electrification was one thing; leaving behind delicacies like the original marshmallow sandwich would have been much more difficult. One can just imagine their mindset: I can leave behind my house; I can leave behind my job; and, I can leave behind my friends, but I am not leaving behind my MoonPies. Such sentiment explains how the popular snack followed the workers to both Detroit and Chicago, quickly becoming a staple snack food in the commissaries, markets and vending machines serving industrial workers. The MoonPies were shipped north by the truckload to bakery partners that sold and distributed the product in a given area one store at a time.

Even with the market expansion of the late 1950s, the MoonPie still had to compete with some rival knockoff products that boasted similar qualities but never captured the taste and recognition of the original pie. In northern regions of the country and the Midwest, a similar snack called a "Scooter Pie" began to claim shelf space. It is no longer made but had been produced at the time by Nabisco, and one-time connoisseurs of the Scooter Pie say it only resembled the Moonpie in size and general composition, meaning it had marshmallow and cookie as base elements. But the ingredients were not the same and the Scooter Pie was baked differently, as well, resulting in a completely different snacking experience for the consumer.

There was also the "Wagon Wheel" in Canada and England and the "Whoopie Pie" in the northeast United States, but none of these products had either the heritage or flavor to endure, and so, ultimately, the knockoffs faded away. This was for good reason, in my opinion, as I recall eating an imposter occasionally in my childhood; these snacks were more of a chore than pleasure to eat since they did not resonate with the same harmony found between the layers with which I had grown accustomed. The differences were as stark as comparing a greenhouse-grown tomato picked in January to one freshly plucked from a garden vine in the dog days of July. They are both tomatoes, but all other comparisons stop there.

Still, even in light of the product deficiencies, the fact that other marshmallow sandwiches even existed in the marketplace kept pricing pressures on the company and its core product, limiting creativity and growth. Now costing a dime, the MoonPie was still a value, but to see the retail price rise only five cents after more than thirty years of production was problematic for Chattanooga Bakery. The company desperately needed to raise the price, but charging more than a dime for the original snack was viewed as too drastic and awkward of a jump, one that might create more inroads for imposter products.

There was also another challenge mounting against the MoonPie. By the end of the 1950s, vending machines were becoming increasingly popular. And not only were they more prolific, but the size of the slots in the machines, which held the snacks, had changed. Made to hold everything from honey buns to longer candy bars, the new vending machines posed a significant problem for Chattanooga Bakery: the MoonPie was in jeopardy because it was too slim and short in diameter to fit into spaces in new vending machine spaces. The snack that was "as big as the moon" needed additional thickness or it risked leaving behind a generation of devotees and becoming another half-baked has-been.

This is the point in business in which companies, or products, either change or suffer a slow and painful death.

Chattanooga Bakery was completely exposed since it had dropped all of its other products, a decision based on knowledge Sam Campbell III had learned in business school: how "to read balance sheets from bottom to top." The MoonPie was the most unique product ever attempted at the bakery, and people "kept coming back for it again and again." Thus, the marshmallow sandwich was more profitable than ordinary, run-of-the-mill crackers and cakes, making it sustainable. But its future was jeopardized when these new types of vending machines threatened to leave it behind.

The saying, "If it doesn't fit, don't force it," often applies to business decisions, but the consensus at Chattanooga Bakery was that the MoonPie belonged in vending machines throughout the country; they just had to figure out a way to make it work. Fortunately, for lovers of the original marshmallow sandwich, the company found a solution that actually created more consumers of the snack and allowed the bakery to charge a higher price point for its snack for the first time in years. This success dates back to the early days of employment of John Kosik, a former company executive that spent more than thirty years of his professional life promoting and selling MoonPies.

A Chattanooga native, Kosik went to work in management at Chattanooga Bakery after completing military duty. He had only been on the job for a year or two in the mid-1960s when it became apparent to all that something had to be done to get the MoonPie into the new vending machines. Kosik was out in the field, traveling with a broker for the company and searching for solutions to the vending challenge, when the idea for the Double Decker MoonPie came to him. It was a moment of epiphany, much like the revelation Earl Mitchell Jr. had in creating the first marshmallow sandwich more than a half century before. Because it was too skinny, the original Single Decker MoonPie was slipping through the vending machine slots. Well, thought Kosik, we'll just add on another layer of cookie and marshmallow.

"It was just a fluke," Kosik says. "We were looking at the pastry machines, and we could see that the slots were only so wide. But they could hold the honey bun, and it was fat. So I said, 'Well, maybe we can get something fat in there.'"

On the spot, Kosik actually drew a picture consisting of a cookie and marshmallow, layered with another cookie and more marshmallow, and a third cookie on top. When he returned home from the trip that evening, he wrote a letter to the sales manager of Chattanooga Bakery suggesting the company consider making his concept—a double stacked MoonPie. Like most great inventions, the Double Decker MoonPie was met with much skepticism. Its main critic was the sales manager, a more seasoned employee, who was much older than Kosik.

"His only response," Kosik remembers, "was 'I got your letter, boy.'"

Despite the sales manager's rejection, Kosik would not let the idea go away, believing it was the most sensible and doable solution to a significant problem. Unwilling to give up on the double-stacked MoonPie, Kosik wrote the sales manager again, drawing and sending along another illustration of the pie with a message that vending was getting bigger and bigger and that Chattanooga Bakery was going to miss out completely without a product to compete. On the second attempt, it gained enough attention that company owner and president Sam Campbell III was presented with the idea, and serious discussion about making a Double Decker MoonPie began.

Calling in the company's production supervisors to talk about feasibility, Sam Campbell III wanted to know if such a concept was possible from a production standpoint. If the company could not make the new sandwich cost effectively and in a timely manner, the double-stacked notion was worthless, even if it could fit into vending machines. Tinkering with the assembly process would prove risky since the bakery had just one production line.

"We were all sitting in the room," Kosik says, "and all the problems were listed as to why it would be difficult. I told them we really need to make this pie, and Sam Campbell [III] finally said okay. He knew something needed to be done and made the call.

"The question then became how. But we had some of the most talented people in the baking business in Fred Stuart and Jimmy Sanders. The idea was to make some samples, running the product through the same line, but capping every other one. Then, we would pick the capped one up and put it on top of the other."

The company sales manager that Kosik first approached about the idea was still not sold on the Double Decker, telling to anyone who would listen, "That boy is not going to be around here for very long." But beginning with a slow, methodical pace that actually doubled the time of production, Chattanooga Bakery made some samples and took the Double Decker MoonPie to market through its sales force. A customer in Columbia, South Carolina, made the first order, asking for thirty cases of the double-stacked product. It did not take long before that first customer asked for a reorder, meaning consumers were responding.

However, Chattanooga Bakery was challenged with the production of the new item, and the sales force moved slowly in response, placing it with new customers at a manageable pace. One new Double Decker customer was added here and another there, but the payoff was that most all reordered rather quickly—more quickly, in fact, than orders for the original MoonPie were coming in.

As the Double Decker orders grew, Sanders and Stuart ramped up the machinery concurrently, figuring out ways to custom build a line that allowed for speed in creating the double-stacked snacks. It was not an easy task, considering most bakery equipment for specialty products is custom built from start to finish. The creation of a machine to double-cap a MoonPie, in many ways, is comparable to some of the world's better inventions. Human hands can rather easily squirt a dollop of marshmallow on a cookie, place another cookie on top, squirt more marshmallow, and cap all this with another cookie. But getting a machine to perform like this, and in a hurry, proved to be a significant challenge at Chattanooga Bakery.

"There was nothing easy about it," remembers Sam Campbell III. "To get it right, one has to go on top of the other. We had to manufacture equipment to get it there, and this took two years. It was a long, difficult process."

Sanders, a Chattanooga Bakery employee for more than forty years and now retired, got the job done by working almost around the clock, seven days a week, tweaking the equipment until the line synchronized. "We had an auto-mation problem," Sanders recalls, "but finally, it just came together. Usually, they would give me the idea, and I would figure out some way to get it done. It all began with a desire for the product. It came down to the fact that something had to be done to make it, and you wanted the least amount of resistance, and the (product) quality had to be good."

The company was still using hand-stackers at the time to straighten misguided caps, and the system was far from per-fect in manufacturing terms, but Double Decker MoonPies began rolling off the line by the thousands. Customers from Charlotte, North Carolina, to Detroit, Michigan, were making new memories with their favorite snack one double-stacked bite at a time. It was a positive scenario for both the company and the consumer because the larger MoonPie sold for almost twice as much as the original Single Decker, meaning that Chattanooga Bakery finally broke out of its long price-point hindrance.

Customers were winners as well, getting a full three ounces more of the product. Priced at less than a quarter, the Double Decker was merely a continuance of the MoonPie's long-standing value proposition. What's more, the Double Decker MoonPie solved Chattanooga Bakery's vending dilemma as it fit perfectly into the new machines, quickly becoming a featured pastry product in most markets.

In Detroit, for instance, hungry and price-conscious workers wanted snacks that were affordable, filling and flavorful, but did not slow them down. The bigger MoonPie apparently hit just the right spot as it became one of the most popular and requested snacks in automotive factories. A result of such popularity was that the Double Decker comprised fifty percent of all Chattanooga Bakery sales within just a couple of years. The increased revenue and market presence was a critical turning point for the bakery, as well as the long-term future of the original marshmallow sandwich.

"Looking at some company financials from way back then," says Sam Campbell IV, the current president of Chattanooga Bakery, "it became apparent they needed to break out of some price points. The MoonPie was a dime snack forever.

"The Double Decker was a real homerun because our big pie would not fit in vending machine, and this form allowed us to charge a new price. But the best part was that the customer was actually getting more, for less."

In business circles, that is called a win-win proposition. But in relation to the original marshmallow sandwich, be it employees of Chattanooga Bakery or consumers, it simply meant mo' pie—which is all that really mattered.

All in the Family

↓

"The Moon Pie is a bedrock of the country store and rural tradition. It is more than a snack. It is a cultural artifact."

—Dr. William (Bill) Ferris, faculty member and senior associate director of the Center for the Study of the American South at the University of North Carolina

IF THERE IS ANY unique characteristic of the MoonPie outside of ingredients, how it is made and a love involving millions of consumers, it is undoubtedly that the brand has been owned, managed and maintained for so many years by three generations of just one family. There are very few legendary companies and products that are still privately held and family-owned; others that come to mind may include such stalwarts as Louisiana-based Tabasco, owned by the McIlhenny family, and E. and J. Gallo, the California winery belonging to the Gallo family.

For three generations, Chattanooga Bakery has been owned and run by the Campbells of Lookout Mountain, Tennessee, a remarkable fact considering the vast majority of family-founded, brand-oriented companies started in America in the early 1900s have either long since been acquired or ultimately closed. Making the Campbell family's association with Chattanooga Bakery even more intriguing is the fact that the company has just one product, the MoonPie.

In talking with members of the Campbell family from two generations, it is obvious nobody ever intended for it to be this way—a monogamous relationship of decades with one solitary snack—but over the years it so happened that no matter how hard family members tried to find or create diversion, the MoonPie always remained the center of both their attention and affection. There was the bakery in Illinois, which the company owned not too many years ago, that made pizza crust, but it was sold, and there have been periodic bouts with baking other private label items. There have also been dozens of other products the family has looked into and considered acquiring or making from scratch. In the end, however, it has come down to a matter of individualism.

"We have taken a conservative approach," says Sam Campbell III, the second generation leader of the family company. "Everything we have looked at or tried outside of the MoonPie has been 'me-too'. If it is not unique, it is me-too, and there are a lot of bankrupt companies in this world making me-too products."

For the generations of consumers who have devoured literally billions of the original marshmallow sandwiches, it has obviously been a good thing since the product today, save some ingredient and baking improvements and the addition of more sizes and flavors, has remained true to original intent and composition. The result is a long and continuous history of reliability, adoration, and experience that strings from one era to the next without interruption. Like a comfortable shirt or favorite hat, it has not mattered to buyers how many other options have been available throughout the years; the one people have been coming back to time and time again is the MoonPie.

Had the Campbell family not held the original marshmallow sandwich so dear, it might not have been that way. It is a troubling thought, I know, but a point well worth making. Just imagine, for instance, if the MoonPie brand had been bought decades ago by a conglomerate food producer, experiencing the same fate of most other leading consumer snack foods that are now lost among dozens of other products. When times got tough, like they did in the early 1960s when vending machines threatened to leave the original marshmallow sandwich behind, what would the conglomerate have done?

As it has been proven, only a family-owned company, with unusually dedicated employees and a close-knit work environment, would have struggled for more than two years to find a way to build the bigger snack. A much larger company, on the other hand, with many products on which to hang annual revenues would probably have taken the easy route, eventually allowing other products to overshadow the MoonPie.

The explanation told in the corporate boardroom justifying the snack's demise would probably have gone something like this: "The MoonPie was a feisty fellow, feeding hungry miners and making finicky children smile, but all great things must come to an end. The larger marshmallow sandwich is just too hard to make."

We can all be thankful history did not play out that way. Instead, the snack remained in the hands of the Campbell family, and they stood beside it, in good times and in bad, guiding it safely through prolonged crises such as times of war, changing tastes and production complications. And along the way, three generations—children, parents and grandparents—have become loyal devotees of the snack, paying Chattanooga Bakery billions of compliments.

"That's the thing," says Sam Campbell IV, "that keeps us humble. After all these years, people out there still like them and keep coming back for more."

I found through research and the prying but genial interrogation of many involved with the MoonPie that a primary
reason consumers keep coming back again and again is the sin-
gularity of attention the snack has received since its creation
in 1917. This has come not only from the Campbell family, but
from the entire Chattanooga Bakery family of employees, most
of whom have worked for two, three or even four decades, and
they have cared for the snack much like a mother dog looks
after a solitary pup, providing protection as well as nudging
nurture, making all the difference in its long-term survival.

But just as most all rewarding experiences have trying
moments, doting over the snack has not always been easy—
far from it, in fact. With the company now in the hands of
his able sons, Sam Campbell III can still remember working
at Chattanooga Bakery in the summertime beginning when
he was fourteen-years-old. Located at the old King Street
location in Chattanooga, the bakery was making five items
at the time: vanilla wafers, ginger snaps, graham crackers,
MoonPies and a round club cracker.

His father, Sam H. Campbell Jr., was running Chattanooga

Bakery, but dealing with health problems, he wanted his son to learn every aspect of the family-run business, a just-in-case type of situation planning for the future. It proved a wise decision, since Sam H. Campbell Jr. died suddenly when his son was just fifteen. The responsibility of inheriting a family business at the time was enormous, but not completely overbearing since Bobby Jones, his father's partner, was still actively involved in Chattanooga Bakery. His temporary oversight of the company allowed Sam Campbell III to complete high school and attend the prestigious Wharton School of Business at the University of Pennsylvania.

There, he studied business, and because it was obvious he would soon be running a family company, professors took a deep interest, serving more as professional tutors than classroom teachers. They taught Sam Campbell III how to read financial statements by reviewing actual reports from Chattanooga Bakery, a kind of apprenticeship that allowed him to learn through direct application. Commuting back and forth from home every ten days where he checked on both the family and the family's business, he balanced responsibility and education, working toward an imminent position of management at the bakery.

Times were somewhat difficult for young Sam Campbell III considering he had a younger sister at home, and it would also be a long time before the discovery of the Double Decker MoonPie alleviated significant pricing pressures in a competitive marketplace. Therefore, it was hardly as if he were a Ford or a Rockefeller about to step into a multi-million dollar empire of industrial inheritance.

With Chattanooga Bakery in the 1950s, work revolved more around duty than glamour, and service came before self. Sure, the MoonPie was quietly becoming a Southern comfort food, sparking one memory after another, but the bakery to young Sam Campbell III was little more than a necessary means, a business to provide for his family. And the responsibility he had inherited as a young owner upon his father's death would become far more serious when Bob Jones died unexpectedly in a car accident, leaving him solely responsible for Chattanooga Bakery and the MoonPie.

Having been drafted into the United States Army following

graduation from college, Sam Campell III was provided a hardship discharge due to the death of Mr. Jones, and he returned home to Chattanooga to work at the bakery. The good news was that there were eight or ten department managers at the company with thirty or more years of experience each, so from a daily execution standpoint, snacks got out the door, and the product was involved in a long-term process of continual improvement in order to diminish marshmallow sandwich competition.

Of the long-time employees making a difference, one that helped Chattanooga Bakery significantly separate the MoonPie from knockoff competitive products was the company's baking manager, Mitch Schauf. Beginning work at the bakery in the 1930s, he was hailed by Sam Campbell III as one of the "best technical baking managers" ever in the American baking business. Under his direction, improvements were made so that the MoonPie was easier to produce and stayed fresh longer.

The secret involved cookie dough that was easier to work with and a marshmallow mixture that joined with freshly baked cookies in perfect union. That is not difficult to imagine, I know, since marshmallow and cookies go together like rice and gravy or peanut butter and crackers, but it was more than complimentary flavor that made the biggest difference for the improved marshmallow sandwich. In a sort of osmosis, the moisture from the new marshmallow flowed to the cookie in a finished sandwich, which bonded the two in a long-lasting, fresh balance that is unequaled in the snack food industry.

"The marshmallow technology was the real secret," said Sam Campbell III. "He developed a product that could stay soft for months, and nobody else could do that. [Schauf] did little things that made a big difference, and he really perfected the MoonPie, improving it substantially over time."

Schauf retired the first year Sam Campbell III was on the job, running Chattanooga Bakery, but his son-in-law was groomed as a replacement, and he served as baking superintendent for thirty years. Continuing the family's contribution, he helped Chattanooga Bakery mechanize the application of marshmallow, leaving behind the original method—dollops dropped from bags which were held and squeezed by hand. Such mechanization was a difference-maker in terms of jumping ahead of the competition since the other companies were making multiple products and, in turn, not spending each and every day searching for ways to advance marshmallow sandwich-making.

As a result of the improvements in product and process that occurred over time, Chattanooga Bakery watched the MoonPie establish marketplace preeminence, leaving competitors like the Scooter Pie in its wake; indeed, the original was establishing itself firmly as the one and only. Internally, the private label marshmallow sandwiches were dropped from production, as were the handful of other items that had previously survived elimination. And a large part of this was due to the work of one man and his son-in-law—two generations of one family involved in a half century of perfecting a single snack.

It may seem strange that a long-time company employee apprenticed a son-in-law before handing over his job upon retirement in the same way company owners groomed sons and passed along knowledge in preparation of jobs in the future, but in reality, it is not. Not at Chattanooga Bakery, anyway. From its very beginning, the MoonPie has very much been a generational family affair.

In the same manner, affinity for the snack has been passed along by consumers, from parent to child and grandparent to grandchild, as if it were a treasured heirloom. And so it is not surprising that company employees have extended the legacy of the original marshmallow sandwich among their own family members. Most employees have worked long-term, as Chattanooga Bakery boasts an exceptionally long average of years worked by employees, and many have been related, resulting in a clannish culture where love and appreciation of the MoonPie run deep. Most seem to understand their work involves something much larger than themselves, the Campbell family or Chattanooga Bakery; it is the daily proliferation of an icon, the memory and promise packaged with each individual snack. That is why over the past fifty years only one company manager has had to be let go.

"The idea," says Sam Campbell III, "is that if there are

only good apples in the barrel, you don't end up with a bunch of spoiled ones. And the good ones tend to attract other good ones, keeping a great thing going."

There is no better example of this, perhaps, than the Sanders family of Chattanooga, which, combined over three generations, has worked for more than three-quarters of a century at the bakery. You will recall from the previous chapter how longtime plant engineer Jimmy Sanders designed and built the baking equipment needed to produce the Double Decker MoonPie. In company lore, he is credited with a feat that is akin to Thomas Edison's invention of the light bulb. It did not happen easily or overnight, but by tweaking and changing and ingeniously creating, Chattanooga Bakery eventually ended up with a fully automated process to produce millions of original marshmallow sandwiches.

This fact was fascinating enough when talking to Sanders, but what perhaps captivated me the most about the man, and the Sanders family in general, was learning that not only had he worked at Chattanooga Bakery for more than forty years, but his father had been a company employee for almost twenty years, while his daughter, Beverly Sanders, is a current employee who has worked thus far for more than fifteen years. Strung together, the Sanders' MoonPie experience is almost equal to the age of the snack itself.

"I came to work in 1947 and just retired seven years ago," says Jim Sanders. "My father was here for five to six years in maintenance after I came to work. He said that he would stay just long enough to get me straightened out.

"Even when he retired, it was still like a family working here. I knew the name of every single person that worked on the production line, and I was in the plant virtually every day."

Romanced by the baking industry because of its uniqueness in process and product, Sanders was not only a tireless worker in his long career—known for working almost around the clock in times of need—but also a devoted fan of the MoonPie. Every year at Halloween, for instance, he would bring the snacks home for the Sanders family to hand out to trick-or-treaters. And on summer family trips, he always carried original marshmallow sandwiches to give away to folks he encountered along the way in Johnny Appleseed style.

Met somebody nice at a gas station? Here, have a MoonPie. Got good service from a hotel maid or host? Here, have a MoonPie. The tradition so struck his daughter, Beverly, she now takes MoonPie's along on trips as well, serving as a goodwill ambassador for Chattanooga Bakery wherever she goes. But some company insiders might think that such goodwill is merely her way of trying to make up for a past transgression.

It happened innocently enough, but few have forgotten and are quick to retell the story with a laugh and affectionate nod toward the culprit. As the recounting goes, Beverly Sanders was at her desk working near the end of one day when a telephone call was patched through to her desk. She took it like any other call and began answering rapid-fire questions about the MoonPie. "Yes," she reponsed, "people love it—have for decades . . . Yes, it is a one-of-a-kind snack . . . No, actually, I don't much care for them."

The man on the other end of the line, a journalist working for a large national publication, thought maybe he had heard her wrong. "What? You don't like MoonPies?"

"I don't eat them," she said. "It's the marshmallow. I'm anti-marshmallow."

There was a brief silence on the line. Even the journalist was stunned.

Stop the presses. We have a big scoop. Dateline, Los Angeles: CHATTANOOGA BAKERY EMPLOYEE DOES NOT LIKE MOONPIES.

Her surprising quote was, of course, used in the story with prominent mention made of the employee of the single-product company who did not like the product. Now, thousands and thousands of readers knew her as an "anti-marshmallow" bakery representative. Beverly Sanders thought she might lose her job over the statement. At some companies, perhaps she would have. But Sam Campbell IV likes to remind himself and others that if you are in the business of making and selling a fun snack like the MoonPie, you have to be willing to laugh more than a little. As he has said before, "I do not ever want us to take ourselves too seriously around here. The brand is special, but it is not steel or cars that we are making, but MoonPies. It is whimsical, and we need to always remember that."

Instead of a pink slip, Beverly Sanders got a copy of the news story taped to her office door with the quote high-lighted in bright yellow marker. Fellow employees—Campbell included—laughed and laughed again about her brush with infamy, and the story remained on display for several years in the hallway of the company's administrative offices. A result of the incident was that she tried the snack again in an attempt to squelch the laughter, and to her surprise, the marshmallow in the middle was much more enjoyable to the palate. After gaining the taste for MoonPies, she appro-priately took the story clipping down. Still, her father jokes about the incident at every opportunity.

"[Company ownership] took it well," says Jimmy Sanders, grinning, "but I tell her all the time she probably missed two or three raises over that one."

There are other instances, of course, when the familial atmosphere of Chattanooga Bakery trumped all reasonabil-ity. The anecdote Sam Campbell IV tells, which sums up the working relationships perhaps better than any others, comes from a retirement party some years ago for an employee who had worked at the company for more than forty years. All of the key company management personnel, including Sam Campbell III, president at the time, were in attendance, toasting her contributions to Chattanooga Bakery.

In the light-hearted spirit of the moment, some of the managers began to joke out loud and snitch on each other about how much in money and items they had taken from the company through the years. It was all true, of course, but admitted in jest. Also, individually, the amounts sounded small, nothing more than something to laugh about. But the stories went on and on, getting bigger as they went, to the point that if someone had been running an adding machine tape, the jokes would have stopped abruptly.

"Dad was sitting over there and listening," says Sam Campbell IV, "and he could have taken it one of two ways. He could have gotten mad, which seemed logical as the owner of the company. But instead, he took the approach that, 'If I'm sitting here now and have survived it all, it can't be that bad.' So he laughed along with them."

It is one of the perks of a family-owned private company

where loyalty and generational ties thrive to be able to openly celebrate the victories, both inside the office and out, mourn the losses, communicate honestly and even laugh when needed. But such camaraderie is the easier part of the family-owned business equation. The more difficult challenge year-after-year is actually remaining a family business, especially when it revolves around a well-known consumer product like the MoonPie.

With such a coveted brand and due to the high costs of the specialized equipment needed to make large quantities of the original marshmallow sandwich, Chattanooga Bakery, by all practical purposes, should have been inhaled by a larger food company years ago. It is a simple law of the land in the brand business that smaller companies with much cache just about always get bought out by larger ones needing a boost or diversion.

There have no doubt been opportunities for the Campbell family to cash out and take up hobbies in lieu of the hard work and full-time challenges that come with ownership. However, there is something special about this hand-me-down legacy obtained from his father company profit and loss statements and took them back to campus for analysis, just as his father had done years before at Wharton.

"They knew this was my chance to learn through application," Sam Campbell IV says. "They got directly involved, and at times we picked it apart, so I would have something to bring back with me."

Upon graduation from Washington and Lee in 1981, he joined the family business the following Monday morning—"I was getting married and needed to earn some money, so I went right to work." Collaborating with his father and John Kosik, a multi-party leadership group was formed, whereby all three were able to make top-level decisions and execute quickly when needed. The arrangement made Chattanooga Bakery nimble and quick in response to problems.

"It was a little unusual," says his father of the executive arrangement, "but it worked similar to how a brand manager does for a larger company. Our objective was to instill a very efficient design where people did not get in the way of processes."

When Chattanooga Bakery moved in 1983 from its original King Street headquarters in Chattanooga to a more spacious facility on the north side of town, near the Tennessee River, the project was largely undertaken by Sam Campbell IV. By this time, he had recently attended and graduated from the American Institute of Baking. The move was a major challenge since the company had operated in the same building, dating back to its beginning just after the turn of the 20th century.

More than anything, the new location provided much needed extra space. In the original facility, for instance, management offices were on the same floor as the production line, and longtime employees recall how they were frequently told they smelled of baking dough and marshmallow when going into public places after a day's work. The new facility provided a more typical plant setting with production clearly separated from other company areas like warehousing and administrative offices.

With two company executives named Sam Campbell roaming the hallways, employees referred to Sam Campbell

Chattanooga Bakery began in the early 1900s as a subsidiary of the prominent Mountain City Flour Mill. It was originally located on King Street in Chattanooga, Tennessee.

Production line workers make sure freshly-made MoonPies are properly stacked.

ABOVE The beginning of the MoonPie production line is loaded with freshly-made cookie dough.

BELOW Chattanooga Bakery began in the early 1900s as a subsidiary of Mountain City Flour Mill in an effort to put useable leftover flour to good use.

The MoonPie and RC Cola became the "working man's lunch" in the 1950s because each cost just a nickel and were recognized for generous serving sizes.

Chattanooga Bakery began making the Double Decker in the 1960s
in an effort to find a suitable product for vending machines.

ABOVE Demand for multi-packs increased in the 1980s when the MoonPie became a popular item with national discount retailers.

BELOW Sam Campbell IV became the first from the Campbell family's third generation to work at Chattanooga Bakery.

Wal-Mart founder Sam Walton made the MoonPie one of his choice products.

Chattanooga Bakery is a family-affair for
(L to R) Sam Campbell III, John Campbell II and Sam Campbell IV.

III as "Big Sam" and Sam Campbell IV as "Sambo" in order to differentiate among themselves. There was plenty of respect to go around, but few formal salutations were made to the father and son Campbells—they did not want it that way.

Once the 1990s arrived, another Campbell family member began working at Chattanooga Bakery. Like his older brother, John Campbell II was not urged to work at the bakery in his youth, and he was never taught or forced to pay homage to the original marshmallow sandwich. If anything, the snack was initially out of sight and out of mind for the man named after his great-uncle, Chattanooga Bakery's very first manager.

"I never thought about MoonPies growing up," he recalls. "My dad never brought them home. There was one time in school, I remember, when my mother brought MoonPies for a class desert. I was amazed at how many kids ate them, and how they were so excited about getting one, but that was about the only time I even made a connection."

Like his older brother, summer employment at Chattanooga Bakery was something John Campbell II had to want and seek. In the beginning, he went elsewhere. But at the age of sixteen, after three summers cutting lawns and another working in a fast food restaurant, he, too, approached John Kosik about a job in the family's business. Predictably, he was hired and quickly assigned a rather difficult task.

In its new facility, Chattanooga Bakery had extra, unused space that the company planned to grow into in the future. Short term, it was not needed, but the plan was to go ahead and get it ready. With a wheelbarrow and tools, John Campbell II began on hot summer days a two-year project in the facility, which had no air conditioning. The first summer, he removed and hauled out conduit and other materials ripped from ceilings and walls, while the next summer was spent painting the interior and newly-installed machinery.

As a college student at the University of Alabama, he continued summer employment at Chattanooga Bakery, doing everything from scrubbing factory floors to mixing cookie dough in the production facility. Following the multi-year apprenticeship, he assumed a job would be waiting upon graduation, but with no management positions open in 1984, the opportunity never came, much to his surprise.

"My brother," he remembers, "called me in and said, 'Come talk to us about the future.' He had just been to a seminar about family business. I was all excited about coming aboard at Chattanooga Bakery, but my brother said he and Dad felt it was more important to get related industry experience first.

"Talk about a letdown. I was all ready to go. But in hindsight, it was a good idea."

Taking a job with Carnation Foods, which was soon thereafter bought by Nestle, John Campbell II was able to work in sales with multiple consumer food products, gaining valuable brand and product placement experience. Much of his time was spent visiting various retail stores throughout the South, taking note of how represented products were displayed and purchased. It would prove beneficial, since his summer employment at the bakery had mostly yielded knowledge about production. In the field, he was able to learn about sales and consumers.

When a longtime employee died and a management level

position opened at Chattanooga Bakery, a telephone call was made to John Campbell II by his older brother. Summoned home to work in the family business, his return was a natural progression following an important initial career experience, during which he learned everything from how other companies positioned product on shelves to unique concerns of grocery store and market owners. One of his fondest memories, however, involved not the products he was representing at the time, but the one with which he was most intimately involved.

"I was working in a store in Alabama one day in the dog food section," he says. "I was down on my hands and knees when a lady walked up. I guess she thought I was an employee of the store, so she asked me if I knew where she could find the MoonPies.

"I stood up and said, 'Ma'am, I think I can help you.'"

John Campbell: original president of Chattanooga Bakery, a 1902 subsidiary of Mountain City Flour Mill; died in 1930s.

Sam H. Campbell Jr.: took over leadership of the company in the late 1930s when his brother, John Campbell, died. He ran the company until his death in 1950.

Sam H. Campbell III: returned to Chattanooga after graduating from Wharton School of Business at the University of Pennsylvania to run the company several years after his father died. Retired from the company, but still maintains an active ownership role.

Sam H. Campbell IV: went to work for Chattanooga Bakery after graduating from Washington and Lee University in 1983, first as a management trainee working under his father, before assuming a leadership role first as vice president and then as president, a position he holds today.

John Campbell II: graduated from the University of Alabama in 1989. He worked for Carnation Foods for several years before returning to Chattanooga Bakery to work along with his brother, Sam H. Campbell IV, as company vice president, a position he holds today.

Under Promote, Over Deliver

↓

"It was around 1978 and I was sailing in a 12-foot Sunfish with my friend in the Intracoastal Waterway off the coast of North Carolina. We were hot and hungry and didn't have any money. Lo and behold, we happened to look across the water and a MoonPie was floating towards us. The water must have kept it cool and it was still in the wrapper. There weren't any other boats in sight and there wasn't a store nearby, either. It was just a gift from above."

—Andee Djoboulian, South Mills, North Carolina

I HAVE LONG BEEN fascinated with the strength of brands and the efforts that have been made through the years by different companies to instill one product or one trade name above others. I grew up singing the tune "I'd like to buy the world a Coke" and still drink the beverage to this day, and I'm always game for "another Nutter Butter Peanut Butter Sandwich Cookie" no matter when or where. In my childhood, I wanted nothing more than to trade places with the kid in the "Who's that kid with the Oreo Cookie" commercial, and as I grew up, I chewed Wrigley's Double Mint gum, hoping I would meet and immediately gain the affection of television's Double Mint Twins. We never did meet, which was probably best considering my hair was probably too long for the finely-groomed, form-fitted girls, but I never turned my back on the gum, doubling my pleasure time and time again.

As an adult, I can see clearly now that the mane is gone. Therefore, I spend less time fantasizing over the Double Mint Twins and Suzy Chapsticks of the world and more energy exploring and trying to understand why we migrate heavily to some brands and products, even freaking over some, while others never captivate us despite the best and most creative efforts to grab our quite-divided attention. There have been several valuable lessons learned along the way in my quest to understand what makes one brand or product more powerful than another, and, typically, they have been eye-opening, to say the least. Take for instance John Deere, the world's leading agricultural equipment manufacturer. Several years ago, while writing on the popular company most known for its trademark tractors, I was struck by how connected and respected the brand is with consumers. Say tractor and most people immediately think green—John Deere's signature color.

Conventional wisdom would explain that advertisements bearing the company's catchy slogan, "Nothing Runs Like a Deere," have worked to perfection over the decades. After all, the brand is the undisputed global leader in agricultural equipment with absolute marketplace preeminence. What I learned while spending time inside and around the company, however, is that John Deere is not a brand which was built in the minds of customers through advertising and promotion. Instead, advertising and promotion merely support a brand that charged to the forefront beginning in the 1960s, when John Deere jumped over the competitive quagmire in agricultural equipment by introducing elements of machinery design as a product cornerstone.

The motto "Nothing Runs Like a Deere" rings true for those who love the green machines, but research revealed conclusively to me that it was not until the company added innovative design to its core principles of quality, commitment and integrity that the John Deere brand leapt to the forefront. By now, you may be wondering what tractors have in common with MoonPies; in product, there's no similarity between the companies—one manufactures two-ton machines, while the other makes roughly two-ounce marshmallow pies. But the businesses are closely related in the realm of brand power.

Similar to the method used to build the John Deere brand, television advertising and catchy slogans had absolutely nothing to do with the creation of MoonPie's voluminous, enduring and growing brand power. Perhaps even more startling than the way the world's favorite tractor company has been stamped into the minds and hearts of consumers is the fact that advertising has been so insignificant in the MoonPie's history that the snack has been the beneficiary of only one—that's right, one—consumer advertising campaign since its creation in 1917.

This is a rather shocking statement, I know. It was for me, too. It will baffle and challenge the thinking of anyone fascinated with brand strength or who happens to work in branding and advertising. Just think about it: more than eighty productive years for one of America's best known snack foods and only one legitimate campaign? Where would Campbell's Soup be without "M'm! M'm! Good!" or the Kit Kat candy bar without "Give me a break! Give me a break! Break me off a piece of that Kit Kat bar!"? Well, they would not be mentioned here, that's certain, but probably forgotten along with other nostalgic has-beens. But if I asked you to reach back into memory, going back twenty or thirty years, and recall the jingle or phrase that made you so love the world's original marshmallow sandwich, you will have a hard time.

One does not exist.

"Our whole impetus through the years," says John Campbell II, "has been to produce MoonPies cost effectively, sell them for a value price, and over deliver with quality."

I knew in approaching this story about the life of a snack that Chattanooga Bakery is a small company in comparison to its multi-product competitors like Nabisco and Frito Lay, making big advertising campaigns a major challenge. Nevertheless, the concept remains hard to grasp that MoonPie, one of America's most recognized snack food brands, has for only brief and recent period been mass promoted to consumers in selective regions in its 89-year history. But I do not dispute the facts, especially since I have lived in the South for more than forty years and cannot recall seeing as many as one single television commercial or newspaper advertisement on behalf of the MoonPie. That is because the only bona fide promotional campaign ever conducted by Chattanooga Bakery occurred in 2005, and while I knew about the ads, I did not have the privilege of seeing them since they were limited to the markets of Charlotte, North Carolina; Birmingham, Alabama; and Montgomery, Alabama.

The first-ever television campaign was aimed toward suburban snack-buying mothers in an attempt to remind them that the MoonPie is more than a memory; it is a particularly suitable staple for the pantry, as well as lunch boxes. Outside of these commercials, no advertisements had been placed since the product launched in 1917; there were no advertising efforts linking the MoonPie and R.C. Cola; and no campaign heralding the creation of the Double Decker in the early 1960s. Instead, the entire buzz was generated from word of mouth by the sales force and regional bakeries representing the original marshmallow sandwich.

It is one of the more interesting aspects of the MoonPie's captivating life that the snack has not only endured for so many years, but still flourishes at an all-time high brand strength and product popularity in the absence of traditional media promotion. To have three to four billion MoonPies sold since production began and without the benefit of company-sponsored, catchy jingles proves that the demand driving those numbers has been a result of pure, unwavering MoonPie desire. No subliminal messages dangled in funny, product-absent commercials; no late-night television entice-ments aimed at snack-vulnerable viewers; just seven decades and then some of people craving and consuming Chattanooga Bakery's marshmallow and cookie creation that comes coated in one of three traditional flavors—banana, chocolate or vanilla.

"As far as the brand goes," says Sam Campbell IV, "we may have gotten in the way, if anything, because our fam-ily needed to make a living. If we started out today with a new product, it would be difficult to take the same approach because you would have to have a wad of money to go into stores and buy shelf space and advertise so consumers would go looking for it.

"We've learned with the MoonPie that because of our com-pany's small size, we can't do both," he says. "So our choice is to get to the product to the consumer on the shelf level and rely on the fact they have been doing the marketing for us for years because they keep coming back for more."

A relatively simple concept, yes, but this is the MoonPie we are talking about, and very little else can explain how something so seemingly dispensable on the surface can be utterly irreplaceable, in reality. Some of its brand power must, no doubt, be attributed to the snack's uniqueness. After all, there is nothing else like it, even in regards to the whacky ways it is eaten.

Most candy bars, for instance, are consumed one way, and one way only. The wrapper is torn from the end, folded back, and the bar is inserted into the mouth for bites of varying size. Even a traditional bakery product like the honey bun has limitations in ingestible creativity. A person can either remove the wrapper, eating the bun from one end to the other, or one can opt for a circular trip around the snack, biting off the spiraling layers until nothing remains. But how exciting and memorable can that be, especially when each bite yields the same consistent flavor.

The MoonPie, on the other hand, began inspiring the imaginations of snacking consumers from its very inception, according to a review of memories provided by thousands of customers on Chattanooga Bakery's 100th anniversary. Most related the original marshmallow sandwich to certain people and places, but many recalled specifically all the possible ways to dissect and ingest it, proof that quirkiness in size, shape, ingredients and have each contributed to the MoonPie's curious stature.

Certainly, the most common method is to open the cellophane wrapper, expose one end of the snack and start eating. It is a process I have repeated dozens of times in my life. But evidence abounds that the MoonPie experience is more than just filling and flavor to many people. Take, for example, the round-house eaters, those who take small bites around the MoonPie circumference, where it disappears one round inch at a time. Then there are the sandwich slayers, the ones who peel the layers apart, devouring one at a time in a bold but classic sandwich cookie tradition.

My favorite, however, are the slow pokes, who outnumber all of the others. These are the MoonPie eaters who typically remember the days when a snack was a valued gift, something to be savored because there was never a box of them waiting in the pantry. Dreading the end of a good thing, the slow poke takes one small nibble at a time, punctuated by two or three short sips of a drink, seeking to make the snack last as long as possible. They loathe the moment when gratification turns to sadness, and the MoonPie flavor and filling disappear, so their approach is to stretch this mouth-watering delight over the longest time possible.

"My first MoonPie memory takes me back 35 years to Anniston, Alabama, where we visited my great-grandparents. We would always have a MoonPie treat. We could have our choice between chocolate and vanilla. I would always choose chocolate. I would eat the top crust, then peel the marshmallow center off the bottom crust to eat that before finally eating the bottom crust. I would make it last as long as I could and savor the taste with each bite."

—Carol Rogers, Bon Aqua, Tennessee

Because consumers consider the MoonPie as much an experience as a snack—appreciating the combination of down-home delicacy, size and value that has made it so distinctive from competitive snack products through the years—Chattanooga Bakery was able to build a brand without advertising. And that is a good thing since, with only one product, advertising costs were prohibitive for a family-owned business. Therefore, the emphasis has been placed on producing a quality product and supporting the customers like bakeries and discount retailers through timely and reliable shipments. If anything, Chattanooga Bakery has undersold the MoonPie, practicing temperance with its resale partners and taking an under-promote stance to avoid over-supply. It is a conservative approach that may have kept growth in check at times, but it has also served the company well, keeping customers hungry and looking for the original marshmallow sandwich.

"It has just been a belief that if you heavily promote one year, you have a dead goose the next," said Sam Campbell III. "We've had instances, in fact, when one customer ordered big, and we've called them and had their order cut in half. You can over-promote and oversell, and we've tried to avoid that."

There are exceptions to every rule, however, and the annual Mardi Gras celebrations held on the Gulf Coast have turned into an aberration of excess in Chattanooga Bakery's conservative business plan. The company happily sells and ships as many original marshmallow sandwiches as revelers care to throw and consume. This number has grown steadily at the annual festivities, and this increase is evidence that the original marshmallow sandwich has climbed in popularity year after year since its humble beginning.

Aside from Mardi Gras, there have been and continue to be many traditions surrounding the MoonPie. Some individuals are responsible for starting these customs, like the basketball coach who, after each summer practice, gave one of the marshmallow sandwich snacks to his team's best free throw shooter that day. Another man kept a box of MoonPies in the freezer during the summer. When he went out to mow his lawn, he would pull one out to thaw, so it was waiting on him when he finished, ready to eat. It was his reward for the work.

Other traditions occur family by family, like the one in which MoonPies fill stockings hanging on the hearth each Christmas morning. And then there are those transpiring regionally, such as the annual Mardi Gras celebrations held in Mobile, Alabama, and along the Gulf Coast region of

Louisiana and Mississippi, where the original marshmallow sandwich has eclipsed all other goodies, claiming the center of attention.

"I was at a parade in Mobile, Alabama, when I caught a few MoonPies. I was eating one when I saw a little puppy under a building. It was lying there so pitifully. I went over and gave it some of my MoonPie. It ate this so fast, I gave it more. I returned to the parade, but when I looked down, the puppy was following me, and it has lived with me ever since. If not for MoonPies, I would never have such a great dog."
—Casey Ginder, Mobile, Alabama

The fact that the MoonPie has emerged as a popular throw at Mardi Gras celebrations may come as a surprise to those who thought shiny, colored beads are the most preferred parade toss. But, depending on the specific locale of the parade, they are not beads but MoonPies which the crowds lining the streets wish to catch. In Mobile, for example, the MoonPie rose in the late 1960s as the most popular item thrown by the Krewes and Mystic Societies because the soft, round edible snack was a better treat and also less dangerous when hurled to parade observers. I guess this makes the original marshmallow sandwich the official Mardi Gras toss since the first parade of its kind held in the United States was along the streets of Mobile.

Who knew?

Despite my own knowledge of many things Southern, taken from a lifetime of living and learning in Dixie, and despite my family's Louisiana heritage, even I admit this one caught me a bit by surprise. I thought I was well versed in the celebration of Mardi Gras; after all, I knew that it means "Fat Tuesday," is French in origin, and dates back to the Middle Ages and the observance of Lent. Brought to the gulf region of the United States by settlers and explorers in the 17th century, the first known celebration of Fat Tuesday in North America occurred in Mobile in 1699, and by the 1700s, parades and parties were being held there annually, as well as in New Orleans.

It was not until the 1800s that parade participants began throwing items from floats to route observers, but, of course, they had neither marshmallow sandwiches nor beads. Standing along a parade route in Mobile in, say, 1875, a person was likely to catch simple treats like French-inspired bon bons or trick-prizes, like a small bag of flour which would burst onto the clamorer, covering them in the white powder and eliciting laughs from Krewes float participants. In the 20th century, such shenanigans became prohibited by law, for obvious reasons, and the emphasis shifted to the throwing of beads, small toys and trinkets—and MoonPies.

Today, the original marshmallow sandwich is the most popular tossed item in Mobile. It has been since municipal law was changed several years ago, stating that items flung from floats during Mardi Gras parades needed to be "soft and round." The ordinance even went so far as to say there could be no "foreign-made MoonPies" thrown in the parades. Of course, there is no such thing as a foreign-made MoonPie since the original marshmallow sandwich is only made in Chattanooga, Tennessee. But some cheaper, knockoff marshmallow sandwiches were finding their way from Asia and into the parades.

Not that the imposters confused parade attendees, who know a true MoonPie when they see one, even in the dark of night. Revelers could tell the difference between the real thing and the knockoffs just by the sheen gleaming off the cheap, faux pie wrappers. As a result of such wise detection, piles of the un-originals littered Mobile's curbsides, while children and grownups alike picked through to find the one and only MoonPie.

"For years, we heard lots of anecdotes from Mobile," said Sam Campbell IV. "Mostly, they involved how people along the route could tell the difference in our product and chased after it. They did not want a knockoff marshmallow sandwich and often let it go right on by. They wanted a MoonPie."

Once it was clear the knockoffs had become a nuisance for the city, piling up on curbs unwanted, the law was changed to make sure it is only the original marshmallow sandwich thrown by Krewes and Mystic Societies. The MoonPie has delighted parade participants looking for light, but sought after items to throw.

Since the annual Mardi Gras parades are a highlight for

most all residents of Mobile and the surrounding areas of the Florida panhandle and the Mississippi Gulf Coast, the snack and its tradition have been stamped into the minds of so many that a popular saying has developed. Supposedly, "one is not a true Mobilian unless your first word is MoonPie." The uttering of this first word happens more than one would guess, according to Mobile resident Frank Bolton.

While attending a Mardi Gras parade with his toddler daughter in 1988, he had her seated on his shoulders, so she could see above the crowd and have a better chance of grabbing the thrown goods. The crowd all around her was yelling for the parade's most coveted throw. It was "Moonpie!" to the left and "MoonPie!" to the right. Soon, his daughter began repeating the calls and pleas, waving her arms and belting out her very first words.

"MoonPie . . . MoonPie . . . MoonPie."

"My favorite MoonPie memory was being crowned the first annual MoonPie king at Citronelle's (Alabama) Mardi Gras celebration. To win this honor, I ate two-and-a-half Double Decker pies in sixty seconds.

The Queen (Roma Faye Etheridge) and I had our picture together in the local paper."

—Doug Earle, Citronelle, Alabama

In New Orleans, however, beads have long been the most popular and traditional parade favor; in fact, for many years it was unlawful to throw food from a float in any Crescent City, Mardi Gras parade. One of the stranger legalities in a municipality known for having quirky laws (fire trucks there are legally required to stop at all red lights in times of emergency), the ban on food was ignored by many Krewes member who would hurl a few MoonPies anyway. Even so, the food law was effective enough to keep the snack from overtaking beads in popularity.

However, awareness is now shifting from the color and glimmer of the beads to how and where they are made—in low-wage sweatshops in China and other countries, often by young girls and woman paid penny wages for their labor. The fact remains that the domestically made MoonPie has surged in demand at Mardi Gras parades in other Louisiana cities and Gulf Coast regions, and each year, the original marshmallow sandwich to increasingly becomes the signature throw for some of the oldest Fat Tuesday celebrations in America.

It is fitting, really, for the Moonpie to be at the center of such hullabaloo. Just as Forrest Gump ended up in all the right places at the right time in the eponymous movie, the original marshmallow sandwich ambles along innocently, warming the hearts, palates and stomachs of so many people, one bite at a time. Where were you in the hours after bombs dropped on Pearl Harbor? Somebody, certainly, was soothing their shaken soul by munching on a MoonPie. Where were you when it was reported that Elvis had died? Nibbling on a MoonPie, perhaps? Such is the case with icons. They are not consciously created or pounded into our being. Instead, they almost unknowingly are there, always.

"The only thing I knew," says John Kosik, Chattanooga Bakery's former vice president, "was that we always needed to fill the demand of whatever segment we were in. It did not matter that we did not advertise. The calls came in, and you had to fill the orders."

Sam Campbell IV agrees this is just the way it has been with the MoonPie, the product which finds itself decade after decade in so many of the right places. One day he finally realized the family was charged with caring for something more important than a simple bakery snack; they were looking after a symbol, one of the South's strongest and most enduring brands.

"The first time it clicked to me was about twenty years ago when supermarkets began to charge for slotting space in stores," he says. "In North Carolina, one of our oldest and strongest markets, we found the stores were not charging us. I realized they felt a need to have MoonPies on the shelves . . . that is brand strength."

The MoonPie is so popular in North Carolina, in fact, that its consumption on a per capita basis is nearly equal to the biscuit in England or the tortilla in Mexico. It is also unusually popular in Texas and can be found on shelves in all fifty states in the Union, but Campbell says with a smile that he has doubts about the product sell-through rate in the state of

Washington, suggesting it is "a good thing [the MoonPie] has a long shelf life."

Jest aside, having product sitting on shelves has not been a problem in the South and throughout other parts of the country where the brand has grown in a grass roots style since its beginning. Dozens of folk songs have conjured up the name and image of the snack, and it appears in the pages of countless short stories and other literary works. It was just a couple of years ago, for instance, that Simon and Schuster published the popular children's book *Jimmy Zangwow's Out-of-This-World MoonPie Adventure* by Tony DiTerlizzi. It tells the story of a boy on a passionate search for his favorite treat, the Moonpie. He dreams of going to the moon and finding an endless supply. Ultimately, he takes a soaring trip around the galaxy and discovers that his love of the original marshmallow sandwich is shared universally.

Knowing Chattanooga Bakery's history of little advertising, it should come as no surprise that the product's appearance in song and book are not the result of carefully crafted placement on the part of the company, but pure and simple flattery in the purest form. This kind of cultural appreciation supports the bakery's strong belief that if the product is consistently fresh and full of flavor, consumers will only want more of the original marshmallow sandwich.

It is a philosophy of snack food branding along the lines of, "If you build it, they will come." In other words, Chattanooga Bakery does not spend large quantities of its time and resources telling consumers how great the MoonPie is. They simply try to make it great and keep their customers coming back for more. A conservative approach, without question, but one cannot argue that the under-promote, over-deliver marketing approach of the Moonpie over the past three-quarters of a century has worked.

Consider all of the branded snack foods that have been introduced in this country over the years. There are literally thousands, but only a few, like the Ritz cracker, the Oreo cookie, or Kellogg's Frosted Flakes cereal have endured the test of time, standing on shelves as strong today as ever before. And with several billion sold and a million more a day going out the doors of Chattanooga Bakery's warehouse, you can add MoonPie to this distinguished list.

I might even suggest it belongs at the top since it got there the hard way. I know Frosted Flakes are *"great,"* like I know "everything tastes good on a Ritz Cracker," because the companies that make the products told me so. On the other hand, my affection for the MoonPie has purely been guided by personal experience, and I have been eating the snack and making memories for as long as I can remember, and there are three other generations of admirers who can say the very same thing.

Sam Walton Calls

↓

"I remember the general store my grandmother owned and ran in a small coal-mining town in southern Indiana. The year was 1960. My cousin and I could not wait to run from our grandmother's farm on a sweltering August morning to the little store about a half mile up the dusty, clay road. Bursting through the store's weathered door, we found ourselves faced with a treasure trove . . . barrels filled with ice-cold grape pop and a display case brimming with MoonPies."

—Cindy Sargent, Franklin, Tennessee

LIKE ALL COLORFUL LIVES explored, the MoonPie reveals in its past several critical junctures which paved the way to a flourishing future. One of the most interesting and significant incidents in the MoonPie's history involves a telephone call to Chattanooga Bakery from the father of 21st century retailing, Wal-Mart founder, Sam Walton. In the late 1980s, the MoonPie was somewhat caught in a state of flux. Customer demand remained as high as ever before, but its lifeblood of sales—mom-and-pop grocery and convenience stores—was changing as consumers across the rural landscape increasingly turned to larger, one-stop shopping retail outlets for their value pricing and items in larger quantities.

With fewer sales outlets, the original marshmallow sandwich faced a considerable challenge: it would not matter if customers wanted the snack if it did not have the same availability for purchase as it had in the past. The changing retail landscape created a bit of a conundrum for Chattanooga Bakery, which had conducted business one partner at a time for more than sixty years. But as the regional bakeries consolidated into larger bakeries and as the number of independently owned markets across the country reduced due to the rising costs of running a small business, the distribution model of the MoonPie needed change. A natural starting point for Chattanooga Bakery seemed to be Wal-Mart, the discount chain based in Bentonville, Arkansas, that was in the process of becoming the world's largest retailer. The company had discussions with a Wal-Mart buyer on several occasions, and by the mid-1980s, MoonPies were approved by the retailer as a rotating stock item in its stores.

Just getting into Wal-Mart seemed to be the answer for Chattanooga Bakery at first, but the sporadic placement created more of a tease for customers in a "now you see it, now you don't" kind of way. For Chattanooga Bakery, it was also frustrating that orders ran in abrupt starts and stops, rather than even flow, but the company held to its belief that some relationship with Wal-Mart was better than no relationship at all. A different story was developing in the field, however, as customers, who had seen MoonPies in stock one day, did not understand why they were not there the next. They began to lodge comments with the retailer's service associates.

"We were called an in-and-out item," remembers former company vice president John Kosik. "It meant you had a shot at getting on store shelves four times a year, or once a quarter. It was boom you are in, bam you are out."

Fortunately, for both companies, Wal-Mart's founder had instilled from the beginning a culture of listening. By traveling to Wal-Mart stores located across the country and asking questions of both customers and associates, Sam Walton often detected the little things that make a difference in a successful enterprise. As chairman of Wal-Mart's board of directors, he played an active role for the company, visiting stores on a regular basis, spreading goodwill and returning to headquarters with feedback from the field that was vital for the service-based retailer. Walton was a pilot who flew his own plane, and he loved spending time inside stores, mixing with associates and even leading corporate cheers. Routinely, he would fly from Bentonville to some small town in America where Wal-Mart had a store, land his plane, and call a store manager to come and pick him up. At the store, he would visit for hours, meeting employees, looking over financials, and giving inspirational talks and explaining the value of good retailing.

On one particular day, Walton was at a store grand re-opening in North Alabama when he quizzed a female associate about sales challenges she faced. The associate promptly responded that customers were frustrated that the store no longer stocked MoonPies and would not be getting any soon since the product was in an off-rotation period. A lifelong Southerner with a deep knowledge of Southern brands and products, Walton was apparently struck by the sincerity of the complaint, suggesting that Wal-Mart was somewhat out of touch with its customers. After all, one of the most popular snacks in the history of the world was not available for purchase on a daily basis in their stores.

De-icing spray is a product worth rotating, especially in the South; Halloween costumes are products worth rotating; water skis are products worth rotating; MoonPies, however, have been consumed 365 days a year since the marshmallow sandwich was created in 1917. It was not less pies Wal-Mart needed, but more, and Sam Walton went on a mission to make this happen upon hearing the associates report.

By this period of his life, Walton was recognized as the retail genius of the world. The company was already making significant global impact, and Wal-Mart's advanced customer service and distribution systems were legendary. Even though he had become a successful billionaire, listed annually as one of the richest men in the world, and faced the challenges of being chairman of the board to one of the largest companies in the world, Walton remained involved in the small but important details of retailing, taking interest in the products stocked on shelves and the management of individual stores. So when the Wal-Mart associate explained to Walton that customers were frustrated they could not get MoonPies, he listened closely.

This is the type of information which executives obtain from time to time and often discard or pass along for a less senior company manager to consider, but Walton acted immediately and began looking for a solution. Initial research told him that Chattanooga Bakery was the MoonPie manufacturer.

He got the company's phone number and late on a Thursday afternoon, dialed in to the Chattanooga offices.

"I got a phone call," recalls John Kosik. "It was around five o'clock in the afternoon. This voice comes on the other end of the line and said, 'Hello, this is Sam Walton, and I want to know why we can't get any MoonPies in my stores?'"

More than a bit startled, Kosik explained best as he could that Chattanooga Bakery had been hoping to move the MoonPie from a rotational item to a full-time, fully-stocked item with Wal-Mart, but had thus far been unsuccessful in making this case to a company buyer. Walton, he remembers, sat silent on the line for a moment with no response.

At this point, Kosik starts to believe the call is a late-afternoon hoax. As previously mentioned, Chattanooga Bakery had a long history of enjoying a laugh at the office. The Campbell family is among the more prudent business families one can find, but each generation has brought a playful spirit becoming of the MoonPie to the workplace. While business is business, they have never looked beyond the fact that it all revolves around a marshmallow sandwich. Feeling he was in the midst of a cruel practical joke, Kosik voiced his skepticism to Sam Walton.

"I'm sorry," he said, "but how do I know this is really you?"

"I tell you what," Walton replied. "I'm going to give you the number to this Wal-Mart store, and you hang up and call me back here."

Kosik hung up. When Kosik dialed back the number, a Wal-Mart associate answered.

"I'm calling for Sam Walton," he said.

"Just a moment," she said. "He's expecting your call, Mr. Kosik."

Kosik, of course, apologized to Walton for having doubt. The company chairman was understanding, and then he gave a passionate pitch for Chattanooga Bakery to send a representative to Bentonville as soon as possible to show its wares.

"We've got to get MoonPies in our stores," Walton said.

A meeting was scheduled for the upcoming Monday morning, just four days away. Walton wanted to see a sample display that might work in Wal-Mart stores, as well as a sample of all the variations of the MoonPie being made.

Sam Campbell III and Sam Campbell IV happened to be out of the country at the time, and upon notification, they simply wished Kosik luck at the meeting. It was standard drill in the company's organizational structure in which any of the top managers had the authority to act and react when needed.

The bakery did not have any sample displays, but it did own a couple of Chevrolet Suburbans at the time, and the very next morning after Walton's telephone call, Kosik loaded up one of the vehicles with boxes of product to the point he could not see out the back, and he began a two-day drive to Bentonville, Arkansas. Traveling with Don Leppert, a company sales manager based in Memphis, Kosik and the MoonPies arrived at Wal-Mart's headquarters for the 8 A.M. meeting, held in Sam Walton's office. The company buyer who had previously worked with MoonPie was there, and Walton explained to all in attendance that the top company executives each had three personal products to choose, manage and promote throughout the company. Then, he announced that the MoonPie "is going to be one of mine."

During the meeting, Walton moved around the office

with animation, getting involved in little details like how the display should look in stores, which direction it should face and how much product it should hold. It would be a signature "Sam's Choice" product, and he wanted to personally make sure the deployment of MoonPies was executed in the best manner possible for both the retailer and Chattanooga Bakery. At the close of the meeting, Walton placed an order for something like twenty-three truckloads of MoonPies, or fifteen cases of product per Wal-Mart store—a gigantic order for a company the size of Chattanooga Bakery. Kosik was shaken by the quantity and jokingly asked Walton, "Who's going to pay for all of that stuff?"

"Sam Walton made our day for about six months," says Sam Campbell IV, laughing. "He gave us a big break."

Naturally, MoonPies in Wal-Mart were a success, although meeting demand was a challenge at first. The production line ran day and night in effort to get the order filled on time and keep other customer shipments from falling behind.

"I remember," says Sam Campbell IV, "someone telling Dad, 'This is going to explode.' He said, 'Yes, but we can't make them fast enough.' It was truly a great American business story of the big retailer placing a big order with the smaller family business. We just had to figure out a way to get [MoonPies] out the door."

That they did, and Wal-Mart customers apparently liked the value and enjoyed finding the nostalgic product so readily available. Soon, Chattanooga Bakery was packaging MoonPies in bulk for Sam's Wholesale Club, and Sam Walton started carrying MoonPies around with him on trips across the country, explaining to everyone that the original marshmallow sandwich was his personal feature product. And in the only book ever written by Walton, explaining his Wal-Mart success and approach to business, the solitary color picture in it shows him holding up a MoonPie with a look of pride.

"I attended a black tie affair honoring Wal-Mart's Sam Walton in the mid-1980s. In his talk following dinner, he discussed several techniques used to motivate employees. One was having each employee select their favorite product, learn all they could about it and every day make

sure that product was fully stocked and properly displayed on the store shelves. He then said, 'I'm now going to tell you about my favorite product.' He reached below the podium and pulled out a box of MoonPies, which he proudly talked about as his favorite for several minutes."

—G.J. Snyder II, The Woodlands, Texas

The personal relationship between Walton and Chattanooga Bakery has continued for years since the meeting held on a Monday morning in his office. In fact, just a few days after the initial order was placed, Sam Campbell IV and Walton got well-acquainted and discovered two mutual loves: bird hunting and MoonPie embroidered caps. Their meeting occurred at a Wal-Mart store opening in Kimball, Tennessee.

Campbell had arrived early for the opening and befriended a girl working in Department 1, which contained cookies, crackers and snack foods. He gave her a baseball cap to wear, which was embroidered with the MoonPie logo. When Walton arrived, he went immediately to Department 1 to check on his favorite product, the original marshmallow sandwich. He asked where the MoonPies were. The girl wearing the hat confidently approached him, pointing out the display. Seeing the hat, Walton took it from her head, and removing his Wal-Mart cap, replaced it with the MoonPie hat. He then proceeded to gather Campbell, the girl, several of his aides in tow and the store's district and regional managers in attendance to redo the display, making it look like the one he had crafted a few days before in his office.

The featured promotion continued for six months with MoonPie's on display in all stores as Walton's choice product. During this time, Campbell remembered from their initial conversation that the chairman loved bird hunting and decided to send some hunter orange caps embroidered with the MoonPie logo to the chairman in Bentonville as a way of showing his appreciation for the relationship. A week after the shipment was sent, the Wal-Mart buyer who worked with the bakery called and asked if the company could ship 24 more hats. The buyer explained that the Wal-Mart executive team was meeting in just a few days at Sam Walton's ranch in South Texas, and bird hunting was on the agenda. But there was just one cap remaining of the dozen Chattanooga Bakery had purchased from a local sportswear company.

"I'll see what I can do," Sam Campbell IV said.

He was able to get the hats made in just two days instead of the normal six weeks, and he sent them by overnight delivery to Bentonville in time to be flown to Texas for the meeting.

In recent history, Sam Walton was not the only person involved with Wal-Mart to be struck by MoonPie mania. Soon after the snacks became Sam's featured product, the manager of a store in Oneonta, Alabama, realized the store had accidentally received an over-shipment of MoonPies. Faced with selling the surplus, he came up with the idea of holding the world's first MoonPie eating contest. Sanctioned by the Chattanooga Bakery, the Oneonta Wal-Mart held the contest in the store parking lot on a Saturday morning in October in 1985, witnessed by more than three hundred onlookers.

"I just started telling people that this was the MoonPie-eatingest town in the whole civilized world," recalled then-store manager John Love in the local newspaper, "hoping that someone would start eating them up. It worked."

The winner of the first annual MoonPie eating contest was the football coach of Oneonta High School, Perry Swindle. For eating six Double Decker MoonPies in about ten minutes, the coach received a cash prize.

"That might have been the hardest $100 I ever made," he said at the time.

The MoonPie's unique relationship with some of the country's leading retailers and consumer chains extends far beyond Wal-Mart, of course. There was the time Restoration Hardware featured MoonPies for sale near the cash register of its stores across the nation, and buyers can now find the original marshmallow sandwiches in Dollar General, Publix, Winn Dixie, Kroger, Costco and dozens of other leading national retailers. One of the more interesting and natural relationships is with the Cracker Barrel Old Country Store, a chain that serves both as a restaurant and nostalgic retailer reminiscent of where my grandfather used to take me more than thirty years ago.

Since the Lebanon, Tennessee-based company serves comfort food and inspires warming memories to dozens of thousands of customers each day in its 500-plus stores spread across 41 American states, the MoonPie is a natural store accompaniment, in the way cornbread goes with home-cooked greens or ice cream compliments apple pie. Recognizing the synergy, Chattanooga Bakery was quick to seize the opportunity some years ago, creating special retro packaging for Cracker Barrel that positions the Single Decker snack in boxes promoting the original "Lookout MoonPie" brand alongside such long-time country store favorites as Necco Wafer Rolls, Goo Goo Clusters and Double Bubble Gum.

"A perfect match," says Tory Johnston, current Chattanooga Bakery vice president. "We share many of the same customers, people who appreciate quality and value, but there is something else. It is that memory of rocking on the porch with their grandparents or the smell of fresh cooked food from the kitchen on Sunday afternoon."

Such relationships as those with Cracker Barrel and Wal-Mart have been vital to the growing popularity of one of the country's oldest and most sustainable snacks, but it has meant a change for Chattanooga Bakery, albeit mostly positive. By selling more MoonPies on the larger-scale retail level, Chattanooga Bakery has seen its distribution sources and price points morph through the years. With product sales leaning more toward bulk-box, discounted grouping than individual snacks sold one at a time, beginning in the late 1980s, customers could buy more pies for less and find them available in more places than ever before.

Since most of the larger chains carrying MoonPies have stores throughout the country, the change has signaled expansive growth for the original marshmallow sandwich. Regional bakeries and so-called mom-and-pop stores are still vitally important to Chattanooga Bakery, but beginning with the call from Sam Walton and continuing through relationships with companies like Cracker Barrel and others, the MoonPie has become not just a Southern snack, but an American snack sold in every state in the union.

The MoonPie Shuffle

↓

"*Like most teenagers, I often found the stress of growing up, meeting parental expectations and educational demands to be painful and difficult. But after school, I always looked forward to a Pepsi Cola and a MoonPie. The creamy chocolate just melted in my mouth, while the rich texture of marshmallow added a sweet contrast. Those periods were calming and relaxing. A MoonPie still brings a feeling of peace and comfort to me at age 65.*"

—Barbara H., St. Petersburg, Florida

OH, MY DEAREST MOONPIE, why do I love thee so? Is it because you are delectably sweet? Is it because you are round like a saucer? Or, is it because you are filling, though not quite a meal? A while ago, I decided the only way to find out what tantalized me most about the round, sustaining snack was to examine its composition from the very beginning. After all, this is what I had done during previous research on books about brands like Ford and John Deere. I would never have imagined, for instance, writing about the magnificent, green harvesting combine without seeing its assembly from start to finish. On that particular trip, I was not disappointed.

Custom manufactured at John Deere Harvester Works in East Moline, Illinois, the combine is little more than one piece of steel pegged to another, station by station, until a mammoth, green machine emerges at the end of the line. I likened the process to having a time-lapsed view inside a mother's womb from conception to delivery; a marvelous development. In fact, so awe-inspiring was the experience that I actually witnessed a grown man shed a tear when one of the green monsters rolled off the line.

Talk about the beauty and emotions of birth.

Similarly, I was intoxicated at Ford Motor Company's Rouge facility in Detroit, Michigan, while watching the repeated assembly of the world's best-selling truck, the F-150 pickup. After a lifetime of riding in so many of these vehicles, from the old, basic, functional models made more for dropping hay bales in pastures, to those smooth-riding, Dr. Bubba, driving machines—you know, the kind of trucks meant for impressing girls on a Saturday night and able to leap raging bulls in a single bound, while Beethoven bellows from eight premium speakers in the cab—I could not get enough of the stamping and welding that goes into production. My desire was to cheer and proclaim to all workers, "If this does not prove America is alive and kicking, I do not know what else will!"

But neither the sight of making combines or pickup trucks compared to or prepared me for entry into a somewhat secret land: the production facility at Chattanooga Bakery. Protected by the foothills of the Cumberland Plateau in three directions and the winding Tennessee River in another, the downtown locale of the bakery provides a sort of anonymity as it churns out an endless string of MoonPies.

It could be a place as fantastic and imaginary as Willy Wonka's Chocolate Factory, crowded with legions of Oompa Loompa workers, who scampered around dizzily, as if fueled by copious amounts of sweets and the latest, greatest energy drinks—and nobody would much know. Generally quiet and adorned with only one MoonPie sign in front, the nice-but-understated facility is not the wild and crazy candy factory of dreams, but a tender-loving-care bakery that stands as testament to the original marshmallow sandwich it produces, as many as one million times a day.

Just like Wonka's fictional factory, there are no public tours of Chattanooga Bakery's production facility; only the lucky few get to see and smell and taste the making of MoonPies, since managing a full-time parade of visitors would prove a big challenge for a small company. Besides, there is something about the mysteriousness that comes with closed doors, which the Campbell family likes. It is one thing to provide snapshots, either through words or film, of how the MoonPie is made, but another to show the snack in its disassembled state. As I found and can attest to after several trips from one end of the line to the other, the ingredients may be good individually—and they are—but it is the resulting treat at the end of production that is the rare prize and keeps us coming back for more.

Let us consider marshmallow as an example. A concoction of corn syrup or sugar, gelatin, gum arabic and flavoring, the marshmallow itself is a bit of a complication to me, something that is always available in the pantry, yet I never really know what to do with it. The marshmallow's name dates back to ancient Egypt, when honey-sweetened candy was thickened with sap from the Marsh-Mallow plant, and as a solitary snack, the puffy, fluffy goo is relatively useless, save nights by a hot camp fire.

In other words, I find it needs a companion. That is precisely why I give effusive praise to Chattanooga Bakery: the company puts marshmallow to its best use that I have found thus far. In fact, so important is the sticky substance to the MoonPie that some educated observers suspect Chattanooga

Bakery to be the largest producer of marshmallow in the world.

It was apparent from the moment I donned the required sanitary cap and walked up the stairs and through the door leading from the company's headquarters into its production facility that marshmallow played an important role in the multi-layered snack. As a lifelong eater of MoonPies, I knew this already, of course, but I might have guessed that Chattanooga Bakery bought marshmallow from another source, squirting the pre-processed mixture onto freshly baked cookies. Immediately, however, I would have been proven wrong, since one encounters the large vats of fresh, churning marshmallow at the beginning of the production operation.

The exact recipe of Chattanooga Bakery's marshmallow is kept in a company vault along with A to Z ingredients and instructions for the MoonPie, but company president, Sam Campbell IV, admits there are subtle but important differences between MoonPie marshmallow and the marshmallow puffs consumers find at their local grocery stores. All I know is that smelling the marshmallow in vats and seeing the molten substance ebb and flow was enough to make my mouth water.

Typically, for me to crave a stand-alone, unadorned marshmallow, it has to be burning on the end of the stick with flames big enough to singe the hair off anyone standing by too closely. But all generalizations are out the proverbial window once you step foot in the hallowed production halls of the MoonPie, and so the marshmallow appeared tantalizing, if not tempting, to me, sticks and fire withstanding. Still, no matter how sultry its smell and appearance, it was obvious the large globs of stickiness needed something on which to adhere and co-mingle. Fortunately for MoonPie lovers, the right thing was in the process of being made not twenty yards away inside Chattanooga Bakery's production facility.

"My favorite MoonPie memory makes my mouth water even now. It was the day my daughter and I discovered that putting a banana MoonPie in the microwave is not only fun to watch, but also tasty. We wanted to see what would happen, so we put it in for just a short time. It started to grow before our eyes. The smell, like warm banana pudding,

wafted from the microwave. We rescued the pie from the oven only to end its life with two forks headed for our mouths. It is still my favorite way to eat a MoonPie."

—Karen Hawkins, Fairborn, Ohio

If any element of the MoonPie is most closely related to the earliest beginnings of Chattanooga Bakery, it is the cookie which smashes both sides of the marshmallow, giving it the distinction as a sandwich. Dough that is mixed daily in large vats near the front of the MoonPie production line is made according to a special recipe, which transforms the would-be shortbread cookie into something between a sweet-ened round and graham cracker.

Once the dough is ready for baking, it enters a 250-foot long, gas-fired oven on conveyor belt, and completely baked cookies emerge on the other end. In all, the MoonPie produc-tion line takes about eighteen minutes from start to finish. It is a sight to behold, raw dough sliding into the oven and eventually coming off the line as finished, fully-wrapped original marshmallow sandwiches, and this, perhaps, was the most rewarding element of my snack-worthy research. Yet, what inspired the most awe in me was the knowledge that all the millions of MoonPies produced each week had the same beginning, traveling on this single production line.

Rarely does a bakery producing huge quantities of an item use only one conveyor track, but it is one way the company has kept costs in check, insuring product quality, as well as corporate sustainability. For perspective on this, consider that when noted snack aficionado Steve Almond, author of *Candyfreak: A Journey Through the Chocolate Underbelly of America* (Algonquin; 2004), made his journey to the Standard Candy Company facility, which makes the illustrious Goo Goo Cluster, another longtime Southern favorite, he found that the candy was not in production at the time of his visit. The reason behind this is that to keep lines productive and running, the Goo Goo Cluster is made only on certain days. The rest of the time, the line produces pecan rolls, King Leo stick candy, and many other private label items, which are shipped all over the world.

That does not happen at Chattanooga Bakery. If the

company is open for business, and production lines are in top shape, without the mechanical breakdowns that plague specialized baking lines, the MoonPie will be created again and again and again. Naturally, the process begins when the large vats of freshly made cookie dough are poured in a big lump at the head of the line. From there, the dough slowly blobs forward until it is smashed onto a large baking sheet and then cut to size by a stamping machine. The belt carries the dough into the oven, and it emerges on the other side as solid, wafer-like snacks that would make a good treat on their own, if paired with a glass of milk.

After traveling through a cold refrigeration room to harden, the cookies undergo a dance employees call "The MoonPie Shuffle," where every other cookie is flipped over so that once they are stacked together, the cookies on both sides appear the same, giving customers a true sandwich experience. It was from this point in the production process that I watched the snack take the familiar form I have known and loved for so many years. Passing under a fast-moving dollop dropping mechanism called the "depositor," marshmallow was squirted onto to the top of every other cookie in the line, and a fraction of a second later, another machine picked up the bare cookies and dropped them onto those with marshmallow, effectively creating the sandwiches.

Now that the cookies and marshmallow were joined in sandwich form, they passed through a glorious wall of spraying flavor, either chocolate, vanilla, or banana—whatever the flavoring of the run happens to be. Here, the final coating rained down upon the original marshmallow sandwich like a drenching downpour on an April afternoon; the top layer of the sandwich served as a deflecting umbrella of sorts, where the liquid coating ran off the top on all sides, covering the outer edge of the snack with flavor. While this final layer acts only as a shell to the hearty ingredients within, it still has the sweetness and candy-like flavoring to improve the treat's overall taste, and so it may be considered the crowning moment in the MoonPie's creation.

The first time I witnessed the actual making of the MoonPie, my host kindly put on a latex glove, reached toward the rapidly moving conveyor belt, and pulled a just-completed and still warm snack from the line before it even reached a mandatory cooling zone before packaging. The newly-coated MoonPie was almost hot, and the still-warm flavoring stuck to my fingers. To the palate, it was similar to the experience one gets when a MoonPie is zapped for a few seconds in a microwave, but with one noticeable difference. The cookie, which is always so curiously soft, was crunchy and hard.

The reason the cookie crunched, says Sam Campbell IV, has to do with the cozy and unusual relationship between the marshmallow and cookies in a MoonPie. Shortly after the sandwich is made, moisture from the marshmallow begins to trickle into the cookie so that after a few days, the hardened cookie softens, resulting in the MoonPie consistency consumers find in stores.

"It is a stabilizing effect," says Campbell. "It is part of what gives the MoonPie a long shelf life. I think the product is actually better a few days after it has come off the line when this has occurred."

But I never considered throwing away my hot-off-the-line MoonPie just because its cookies were a bit crunchy. To the contrary, it was similar to, say, kissing your girlfriend's twin sister; different, but nonetheless enjoyable. Not that I have ever experienced such, but one can imagine, right? Anyway, indulging in a fresh-from-the-line snack and watching MoonPie production in person helped me to understand the complexity of the original marshmallow sandwich better than perhaps anything else. Sure, it is just a combination of cookie, marshmallow and flavored coating, items that seem rather non-dynamic individually—implying that a freak like me could be more than mildly insane.

I learned first-hand, however, that there is something more about the MoonPie. Seeing raw cookie dough pour onto the conveyor belt on one end and emerge eighteen minutes later as thousands upon thousands of the neatly-stacked, marshmallow-smashed, fantastically-flavored baked snacks, I gained the perspective that what happens on the production line every day at Chattanooga Bakery resembles more miracle than Willy Wonka madness. Fed furiously into packaging and ready to be shipped into orbit for such planetary destinations as Austin, Texas, and Charlotte, North Carolina, the freshly-made, harmonious MoonPies prove that the little things we know and love in life, which typically seem so simple, often are not.

One Bite at a Time

↓

"As a boy at the age of nine or ten, I lived out in the country. If I had been able to stay out of trouble during the day, I would receive some treat that night. Of all the treats I had as a child, the only one I remember was eating MoonPies into the shape of the evening's moon and holding it up and blocking out the whole moon with my MoonPie."

—Bill Archer, St. Joseph, Missouri

I LEARNED SOME TIME AGO that frequently what one man views as beauty, another sees in an entirely different light. Such became obvious in regard to Chattanooga Bakery's production line as I explained my captivation with the process to the company's president, Sam Campbell IV. When I spoke of the twists and turns and the intricate passages with pure adulation, he responded in tones of guarded respect.

With just one line to produce more than a hundred million MoonPies each year, the slightest problem anywhere along the way can cause major headaches. That is why Campbell and many company employees have somewhat ambivalent feelings when it comes to the highly customized, completely mechanized baking line. On the one hand, the line took years of work to complete, and on most days, it provides exceptional results, churning out product for people from coast to coast. On the other hand, the process has at times been a proverbial thorn in the side for Chattanooga Bakery.

The reason for this, of course, is that the baking industry is so highly specialized. Just consider how many other lines exactly like the MoonPie's exist in the world—zero. A customized invention that has evolved step-by-step since the snack was first invented in 1917, the production line at

Chattanooga Bakery is a wonderment of widgets, belts and bakery equipment that work in sync on most days to create millions of small miracles.

History has shown, however, that some days have been better than others at Chattanooga Bakery, especially in more recent years as they have increasingly relied on automation to improve both product quality and production and cost efficiencies. Customers have been unable to detect any such production problems so far, since MoonPies have remained on store shelves during these times of distress, but there have been some periods in which these minor troubles have reached a critical point, threatening the bakery's schedule of shipments.

The first significant production problem that stands out in the minds of the Campbell family and long-time employees involved the transition from the Single Decker to the Double Decker pie. Adding another layer after so many years of making the traditional marshmallow sandwich came with issues, but they were not overly problematic since orders for the double-stacked product, launched in the 1960s, were made at a manageable rate. The same was true when Chattanooga Bakery relocated in the early 1980s from its original King Street location to its facility near the banks of the Tennessee River. The company needed to remodel its production process because it was outdated, but the Campbell family and company engineers decided against doing this at the time of the move for fear it would be too much change, too fast.

"Around here," says Sam Campbell IV, "we call it eating the elephant one bite at a time. The move was enough change. The rest would have to come later."

Certainly, there were issues with the move, but like the transition to the Double Decker, they were bearable and relatively non-threatening. Seven years later, however, it became obvious that the old way of making MoonPies—with crews taking freshly made cookies off the line by hand, stacking them neatly into boxes, and feeding them into another machine to apply marshmallow—was no longer efficient and something different needed to be done.

"[The system] was covering many ills," says Sam Campbell IV. "We decided to get out of the stacking business and run the line properly, running the cookies straight into a marsh-mallow machine."

Simple enough, right?

Wrong.

Newly-installed equipment did not work well, if at all; and this is a major problem in a business that is, unfortunately, low margin and, therefore, must be high volume for profit-ability. Especially with only one line to run, there is always pressure to keep it going without interruption. But marsh-mallow was being deposited where there were no cookies and cookies were being sent where there was not marshmallow. It was one step forward and about five steps backwards. More labor was needed to essentially hand-make MoonPies so the product could get out the door, while company engineers struggled to find a way to make the equipment work.

"It has taken years of [equipment] tweaking to get the MoonPie right," says John Campbell II, "and it came at the hands of some suffering."

The production by hand was not nearly fast enough, either, not to mention the exorbitant labor costs. As a result,

Chattanooga Bakery suffered several years of financial losses and some strained relationships with partners demanding shipment of back-ordered product.

"It was a huge mess," says Campbell, "but folks kept their head up. The MoonPie had been around for too long to give up. The problem, of course, boiled down to the fact that we had one assembly line. But it is difficult to go from one to two in a family business . . . the machinery is so expensive. Large companies can more easily add lines, but we have to find ways to make it work with what we have."

Consider that McKee Foods Corporation, the maker of the popular Little Debbie snacks that is located just more than thirty miles from Chattanooga in Collegedale, Tennessee, runs more than a dozen baking lines at its production facility. At Chattanooga Bakery in the late 1990s, getting finished product from one line to the warehouse for shipping was quite a struggle. As the financial losses mounted, the company began spiraling, and for the first time, the company with a distinct "anti-meeting culture" held meetings to create a solution. Over time, thanks to the diligence and tireless, around-the-clock work by people like Jim Sanders, the production system was reworked into a start-to-finish flow that began with raw cookie dough and ended with finished product.

Remarkably, Chattanooga Bakery suffered no loss in its customer base, even when some shipping deadlines were missed. There are many has-beens and few survivors in the annals of American baking history, but the MoonPie emerged from its latest trouble unscathed in the hearts, minds and appetites of consumers.

"Many businesses would have been sunk after that," says Sam Campbell IV. "Our customers stayed with us . . . they forgave us. That showed the strength of the MoonPie more than anything else."

Near the close of the 1990s, Chattanooga Bakery's production line was running smoothly again, and with significant growth in its retail distribution partners on both the national and regional level, the MoonPie was reaching more customers farther away than ever before. The management team, by experience, knew that companies which do not go through change will die sooner or later, so they made a critical, albeit dramatic, decision in an effort to keep the snack relevant. Ever since the original marshmallow sandwich was created, the promise of the MoonPie involved both flavor and its large size. Be it miners in the Appalachia, automotive workers in the Detroit area, or children of the South, consumers came back to it because it tasted good and was filling.

For decades, this spurred product growth as the super-size me generation yearned for more food for less money. But Chattanooga's bakery team recognized near the latter half of the 1990s that for the MoonPie to remain appealing to generations in the future, it needed to be made and sold in a size that made sense for mothers to stock in household pantries or school lunch boxes. An eight-year-old, for instance, may love a traditional Single Decker or Double Decker MoonPie, but the full-size snacks can be a bit much volume-wise.

"One of the complaints we sometimes heard from mothers," said Tory Johnston, Chattanooga Bakery vice president of marketing, "is that [full-size snacks] ruin dinner because of the size of the serving. We wanted to take the product down to a size that fit kids aged three to twelve."

The solution was to create a Mini-MoonPie, an exact duplication of the original but in a much smaller size. The idea was to produce a multi-pack option that fit well with large-scale discount retail stores like Wal-Mart and Dollar General and "made sense for Mom."

"We found we were leaving behind a whole generation for the first time," says Sam Campbell III. "We had a multi-pack of single decker product, but we could not break into any new markets. You can see all of these wonderful consumer brands through the years that have ended up as little more than nostalgia. We needed something new that was also the same. The mini is helping us create a new generation of memories."

The timing was perfect considering the MoonPie is a school-approved snack and a good option for children since marshmallow, one of the key ingredients, is fat free. A prototype was developed, marketing materials were made, and more initial orders were taken for the Mini MoonPie than anyone ever imagined. Unlike the Double Decker, which launched quietly and steadily and grew in popularity some thirty years before, the Mini was set to debut amid much fanfare and anticipation. Knowing the snack's popularity, buyers for large retail chains knew the smaller size would strike a chord with shoppers, so they ordered large.

But giving birth to the Mini MoonPie was a painful experience for Chattanooga Bakery. The production line that had been developed more than seventy years ago to make four-inch snacks was going to have to be calibrated to make something half that size. In non-baking terms, that would be like trying to fry eggs on a barbecue grill or attempting to smoke a turkey in a skillet. It may not sound that difficult, but in reality, it was; the Mini marshmallow sandwich came into the world kicking and screaming as a production misfit.

It troubles me to imagine something so sweet as a Mini Moonpie causing such stress and unrest, but that is clearly what happened almost ten years ago when Chattanooga Bakery first tried to bring the little guy to life. Like a breach birth, the new snack held much promise, but there was nothing easy about its delivery. When asked about it, Sam Campbell IV recalls that it was not some days, but most days, that they tried painfully to bring the Mini into the world.

"Pretty much everybody around here got a little more gray hair," he says. "Through the years, we had done everything possible to make our production line more efficient, but what we found out is that it was not flexible at all."

It was the first time ever, Campbell recalls, that he thought about looking for another job. The line capper, or marshmallow depositor, holds the most importance of any element on Chattanooga Bakery's production line. Applying marshmallow on one cookie and accurately stacking another on top, if the depositor does not work properly, there are big problems. The general idea was that the smaller cookies could run through the production line if spaced properly and given less marshmallow.

But, oh, how the best laid plans often fail.

When Campbell watched the first attempts of producing the Minis in large quantity with millions on backorder, he wished he was anything but a MoonPie magnate. A fishing lure magnate, yes; a golf ball magnate, perhaps; but definitely not a MoonPie magnate. The altered line ran as if a wrench had been thrown into the previously smooth-running system.

Single Deckers, Double Deckers . . . everything was thrown off by the Mini MoonPie's attempted entry into the world.

By introducing a product and stacking up orders before the first one successfully came off the production line, the company was in a position to lose a number of potential sales. Chattanooga Bakery could not meet the demand, and employees worked hours-on-end manually making MoonPies by filling in where automation could not function. But they were not making them fast enough, and customers wanting orders complained, some loudly.

"There were so many delayed shipments," recalls Chattanooga Bakery customer service representative Janice Wilkes, "you would have thought we were producing kidneys and hearts."

I reminded her that to some of us, they may as well have been. When a person gets a MoonPie on their mind, well, there is not much they can do about it, production problems be darned. That is probably the reason that, though some customers fussed over the belated orders, very few canceled. And soon enough, after a little more time and a lot of apologies to customers, the kinks were eventually worked out of the system; production got back on schedule; and mothers were able to buy boxes of Mini MoonPies at their favorite retail outlet.

"When something like that happens," Campbell says, "it throws everything off and changes your perspective. Once again, we learned how much customers value the MoonPie because most all stuck with us. They may not have seen how hard everyone was working to get that product out, but in a way, they understood."

Infinity and Beyond

↓

"My favorite MoonPie memory is when I was a small boy living in Middle Tennessee. We had a country peddler that came around about once each week selling kerosene and grocery staples. My mother would swap chickens and eggs for things the family needed. She would sometimes have enough to buy a MoonPie for me and my brother. It was a special treat for me then, and I am still enjoying MoonPies today."

—Dan Foutch, Knoxville, Tennesseee

EVERYBODY HAD HEARD countless times the old adage: "The more things change, the more things stay the same."

I have long considered this to be an exaggeration since not much in my life today resembles anything close to the way it was in my youth. I remember, for instance, when my grandparents finally got off of their party-line home telephone connection. Now, I can hardly figure out how to work the many available features on a micro-sized mobile telephone.

My multiple television sets get so many stations I can rarely find one suitable program. Just more than a quarter-century ago, we only got four stations on an antenna connection serving a single TV set at my house, and all programming seemed worth watching during that time. We live in a time in which our country's elected officials are often ridiculed, while wild and crazy celebrities are revered. Money and opportunity always seems too short in supply, yet everywhere we go, both seem to abound in large quantity around us.

Teenagers have more luxuries at their fingertips than most of us could have ever imagined obtaining in a lifetime, while the elderly, those who have earned the right for a little luxury, often struggle for basic essentials amid health care costs and meager benefits. Vehicles come with satellite and video systems and are bigger than ever before as the supply of gasoline diminishes. People think nothing of paying $25 for a steak, while newspapers costing fifty cents are largely ignored.

But I now know firsthand that there are actually some things in life which have changed very little, if at all. After months of researching and learning about the world's original marshmallow sandwich, I can finally admit the more things change, the more *some* things remain the same. It seems to be one reason why freaks like me keep the MoonPie close by, both in spirit and for consumption. It also appears to be the reason why Chattanooga Bakery is making millions of MoonPies each day, more than three-quarters of a century after a company salesman solved a snacking dilemma for hungry coal miners.

There is no doubt that Americans love to snack, with each person consuming on average something like 20 pounds or more of snack products each year, from doughnuts to cookies to potato chips. But the marketplace is more crowded than ever before, meaning by all practical purposes that a little family brand like MoonPie really should not have been able to come this far. After all, in today's world, it is always out with the old, in with the new. Not surprisingly, there are many who can hardly believe the company's success, even some Chattanooga Bakery employees like Janice Wilkes, a customer service manager, who wonders if the long, good ride might end.

When she first interviewed at the company almost fifteen years ago, the product was in the midst of a significant upward trend, the production line running overtime to meet demand. Wilkes had familiarity with the original marshmallow sandwich, but figured the popularity surge might be a sort of aberration, demand provided by a fickle consumer taste of the moment. When offered a job, she took it because Chattanooga Bakery seemed like a nice place to work, and she could get in on a good thing, while it lasted.

"I was a skeptic," she recalls. "I thought, 'I will just ride this wave out as long as I can.' But it turned out not to be true, because this product and this brand is bigger than all of us."

Time-tested and true to its original promise, people like me have been going back to the MoonPie for generations because it is a known and trusted entity, providing a wealth of happy experiences to recall, from overwhelming flavor to filling satisfaction. It is a comfort food, keeping us relaxed in an otherwise fast-changing world. And it has the power to stir in us our most poignant memories. One particular lover of the original marshmallow sandwich is led to remember how her daddy took her to the store as a young girl and let her choose a MoonPie. Instead of flowers, she now takes the snack to his grave when she visits. And the MoonPie is also a contemporary food, as parents and grandparents continue to pass their love of the pies along to children.

Through the years, most changes at Chattanooga Bakery and with the MoonPie have been so subtle that consumers probably never even noticed them—a tweak to the cookie dough here, a new flavor sprinkled there. Only the introductions of the Double Decker in the 1960s and the Mini in the 1990s garnered significant public attention, but these were merely differences in produce shape, not flavor. The marshmallow, the cookie and the coating have basically remained the same since the first MoonPie made in 1917.

At the same time, the bakery has always strived to make the pies better, using the best available ingredients and providing customers with more choices. Even when asked about the future, Sam Campbell IV says the prospects for great change in the snack are slim. Maybe more advertising, perhaps some expansion in product flavor and package offerings, but Chattanooga Bakery plans on making the original marshmallow sandwich in much the same way it has for more than eighty years.

Simple in concept, yes, but billions of MoonPies later, it is an approach that has worked, allowing the snack to survive everything from economic depression and recession to world wars and modern diet fads. And more demand exists today than ever before. Consider only that the Mini MoonPie, developed less than eight years ago, now comprises twenty to thirty percent of Chattanooga Bakery's total business. By meeting a lower price point and giving mothers a choice in product size, the Mini MoonPie is well-positioned along with its orbital counterparts to introduce yet another generation of consumers to the goodness.

Appendix

MoonPie Facts

↓

↓ Chattanooga Bakery makes on a regular basis MoonPies in three flavors, including banana, chocolate and vanilla, while flavors such as strawberry and orange appear seasonally. Chocolate, however, remains the most popular, consisting of more than fifty percent of sales in the Mini and the Single Decker and Double Decker pies. It is most popular in grocery stores, as opposed to convenience stores and vending machines, though nobody is exactly sure why.

↯ The MoonPie has been used as an ingredient in ice cream on numerous occasions. The Matterhorn Company, and subsequently, Fieldbrook Farms, made the MoonPie Ice Cream Sandwich. Several dairies have made a special MoonPie flavor ice cream, mixing chunks of graham and chocolate into a marshmallow-ribbon vanilla.

↯ The age group most likely to consume a MoonPie is the 35 to 54-year-old demographic, which consumes one-third of all MoonPies made and sold.

↯ The MoonPie is the original marshmallow sandwich, but many years ago, there were as many as seven competitive brands offering knockoff products, and Chattanooga Bakery itself was making the snacks for five of these private labels. Therefore, it was not unusual to go into a country store in North Carolina in the early 1950s and find five different marshmallow pies, all of which were made by Chattanooga Bakery.

↙ For many years Chattanooga Bakery sold its product in Japan through a licensing agreement with a large bakery there. Because its name made reference to the moon, the snack was a prestigious item used in advertising. Chattanooga Bakery was not able to license its trademark there, however, and the relationship ended.

↙ People often wonder why Chattanooga Bakery is not named after its one and only product—the MoonPie. Members of the Campbell family say discussions have been held before on changing the name, but the consensus has been that the MoonPie is a beloved consumer brand, not a company.

↙ For much of its history, Chattanooga Bakery was known as "a baker's baker," distributing MoonPies almost exclusively through partner regional bakeries. Chain stores were large customers, buying directly from the bakeries and eventually, vending machine sales rose in importance. Then, in the 1980s, discount retail chains emerged as buyers. Over the years, Chattanooga Bakery expanded its footprint, progressing naturally with each opportunity as it came along. Today, the company maintains relationships with bakeries as well as numbers of regional and national customers which stock and sell MoonPies.

↙ Because of the amount of sandwich filling it uses to make more than 100 million MoonPies annually, Chattanooga Bakery is believed to be one of the largest producers of marshmallow in the world.

↙ Many people think of the MoonPie as a Southern snack, but the original marshmallow sandwich has, in fact, been sold and consumed nationally since the 1950s.

↙ Chattanooga Bakery launched its first-ever television campaign in 2005 with a commercial titled, "A Little MoonPie Can Change the World." Run in metropolitan markets that included Charlotte, North Carolina, and Birmingham, Alabama, the ad showed real people going about their typical, stress-filled and over-committed lives. Amidst all the noise, the ad pointed to the "innocence of kids and the simple enjoyment of things like the MoonPie."

↓ The popular consumer association between MoonPie and RC Cola was not the result of marketing efforts on behalf of Chattanooga Bakery. Instead, the well-known link between the two, which emerged through both song and saying in the 1950s, is attributed to all the Southerners who liked the value proposition offered by both products and therefore chose to purchase the snack and drink together.

↓ The MoonPie has a shelf-life of four months, one of the secrets to the enduring snack's success.

↓ MoonPies have been prominently featured in several popular songs, including Lonzo and Oscar's 1951 hit,

"Give Me an RC Cola and a MoonPie," and Alabama's 2001 cut, "When It All Goes South."

↙ Bell Buckle, Tennessee, is a town of just more than 400 residents, but each year more than 20,000 revelers arrive to celebrate the MoonPie. Located about fifty miles south of Nashville and just more than ninety miles from the MoonPie's Chattanooga home, Bell Buckle hosts the annual RC Cola and MoonPie festival, which includes a run, parade and the crowning of king and queen.

↙ MoonPies are so popular at Mardi Gras celebrations on the Gulf Coast that several newspapers typically run recipes after the Mardi Gras parades, so households "overflowing with the tasty treats" can make good use of the leftover pies.

MoonPie Recipes

↓

CHOCO-BANANA-NUT MOONPIE

1 chocolate MoonPie
1 banana MoonPie
vanilla ice cream
chopped almonds

Directions: Cut both pies in half. Switch the tops. Now you have two banana-chocolate MoonPies. Sprinkle with chopped almonds. Microwave for 20 or so seconds, until marshmallow begins to bloom. Add one scoop of vanilla ice cream on top. Enjoy!

This recipe submitted by Ethel in Kingsport, TN.

HOT FUDGE MOONPIE

1 chocolate MoonPie
vanilla ice cream
chocolate syrup

Directions: Place MoonPie in microwave-safe bowl. Microwave on high for 15 seconds or until chocolate coating begins to melt. Place 2 scoops of vanilla ice cream over the warm MoonPie. Add 3 tablespoons of chocolate syrup. Eat with a spoon. Enjoy!

This recipe submitted by Joe and Barb from Annapolis, MD.

PEANUT BUTTER MOONPIE

1 chocolate MoonPie
3 tablespoons smooth peanut butter

Directions: Chill MoonPie 2–3 hours in refrigerator. Remove top layer of pie. Spread peanut butter on top of marshmallow. Reapply top layer. Enjoy!

This recipe submitted by Jane Benton, Murfreesboro, TN.

STRAWBERRY MOONPIE SHORTCAKE

1 vanilla MoonPie
4–6 fresh chilled strawberries
whipped cream

Directions: Place MoonPie in a bowl. Use a fork to poke holes in the MoonPie to let the juice soak in. Cover the MoonPie with the strawberries (and the juice), then add some whipped cream. Let sit for 5 minutes (if you can wait that long).

This recipe submitted by a MoonPie lover from Charlevoix, MI.

TURTLE MOONPIE

1 chilled MoonPie (any flavor)
caramel sauce
hot fudge sauce
chopped nuts

Directions: Remove top layer of chilled MoonPie. Pour hot caramel sauce on top of pie, then hot fudge sauce. Sprinkle with nuts, preferably pecans. Eat with a spoon to minimize waste.

This recipe submitted by Paul Zonfrillo, Greenville, SC.

BANANA SPLIT MOONPIE

1 chilled banana MoonPie
1 banana
chocolate syrup
ice cream
chopped nuts

Directions: Remove top layer of chilled MoonPie. Place thin slices of bananas on both sides. Place on a plate and cover with a thin coat of chocolate syrup. Sprinkle with nuts and add a cherry to each half. Be leery of lurking kids or spouse. Retreat to your favorite easy chair and ENJOY!

This recipe submitted by Jim in Carrboro, NC.

MOONPIE BROWNIE

3 MoonPies (any flavor)
brownie mix

Directions: Spray the bottom of a 13" x 9" glass baking dish with a non-stick cooking spray. Line bottom of dish with chopped MoonPies. Pour brownie mix on top of MoonPies. Bake according to brownie mix directions.

This recipe submitted by Daphne Scherzer, Chattanooga, TN.

HOMEMADE MOONPIE ICE CREAM

1 qt. whipping cream

1 qt. + 3 cups whole milk

12 egg yolks

4 tbsp. vanilla

3 cups sugar

2 tsp. salt

4 to 8 MoonPies

Directions: Scald milk in large 6 qt. saucepan. In large bowl, beat together egg yolks and salt. Add 3 cups of the hot milk to the egg yolks slowly while stirring constantly. Then return this mixture to the milk in the pan. Add sugar and keep stirring while cooking at medium heat. When mixture coats the spoon or just starts to boil, remove from heat. In most cases, the mix will be lumpy. Remember to strain out the lumps when you pour it into the canister. Add chopped MoonPies and freeze.

This recipe sent to us by Zane Harris, Charlotte, NC.

Acknowledgements

↓

SHORTLY AFTER COMPLETING most of my work on this project, I ran into a man I had never met but with whom I had a familiarity because of a newspaper article I had recently read. Perhaps the most notorious bookseller of our time, Dewitt Gilmore, who goes by the pen name Relentless Aaron, went from a prison term in 2003 to top-selling author in 2006. Today, he has a multi-project book contract with St. Martin's, one of New York's more respectable publishing houses.

I was immediately intrigued by this man, not only in the way he admirably turned his life around, moving from check-cashing fraud to literary respectability, but because he has an ability to see right to the pithy core of a book. He subscribes not to the stuffy principles of literature, but to the promise of pages filled with mind-opening, exploratory text.

That is why I owe the man known as Relentless Aaron, America's most successful author of the genre known as street lit, a great big thank you. For when he saw the cover of this book, displayed at a recent trade convention, and recognized immediately my idea in writing about the MoonPie, I knew my time spent on this project was all worthwhile.

"So," he said, breaking into a grin, "you wrote a book about a *cookie.*"

A MoonPie is more than a cookie, of course, but that is not the issue here. That Relentless Aaron recognized on first glance my attempt to be a biographer of a revered snack food meant that my work was not in vain. Often, all a writer wants is for one person to accurately understand his or her intentions. Relentless Aaron got *MoonPie* on the first take. For his individuality, as well as his ability to see the world for what it is, I am deeply appreciative.

From the start, all I wanted to do was write a book about

the original marshmallow sandwich. If I have done outside of this, I apologize, since after more than eighty-five years of making memories, the MoonPie deserves to have its story told well. Fortunately for me, many people wanted to help in my attempt to get this tall-but-true-tale right, and the list of those to thank for this includes many.

Belonging at the top, without a doubt, are members of the Campbell family. The proprietors and caretakers of the beloved MoonPie, America's original marshmallow sandwich, they are not only good business people, but good people in general. They approach business with the diligence and respect it deserves, and are highly regarded by employees for steadfast support. They are comfortable in the biggest boardrooms and are also relaxed in the most humble and rural of surroundings—preferably with fishing rods in hand. They are highly protective of the MoonPie brand only because they want it to remain a simple yet beloved snack, able to provide endearing memories for years into the future.

It is for these reasons that I give a personal and heartfelt thank you to Sam Campbell III, Sam Campbell IV, and

John Campbell II—thank you for letting me get to know the MoonPie more intimately, and thank you for being good friends and neighbors.

Also at MoonPie a special thank your to vice president Tory Johnston, a man who is worthy to care for one of the best brands in America. He understood the opportunity of this project from the beginning and has worked to make the job enjoyable along the way.

I have never had the privilege of meeting Emily Ley-Shiley, a native of Chattanooga who graduated from the University of South Carolina, but her documentary "How Chattanooga Mooned America," which was produced while she was studying film as a college student, was an excellent resource and a real inspiration. When Earl Mitchell Jr. is quoted in this project, it comes directly from her documentary. Filmed in 2001, the documentary debuted at the Rural Route Film Festival in New York in 2003. Being able to view her work at the start of this project helped expand my appreciation of the MoonPie considerably. To her, I say thank you.

Appreciation also goes out to Ron Dickson, the man who

wrote the first MoonPie book. The undisputed head of the MoonPie Cultural Club, he helped me with an understanding of the snack and its legions of followers.

At Jefferson Press, Charlotte Lindeman helped conceive of this project and has been a tireless worker in promoting it; Henry Oehmig has provided valuable editorial insight; and Fiona Raven did quite well on interior and cover design, as always. Also, I owe special thanks to Miller Welborn and Paul K. Brock Jr., business visionaries, as well as good friends.

The dedication of this book is to my wife, but that mention alone is not enough. She inspired me to be a writer and gets credit for steadfast support along the way. Truly, without her, no book of mine would ever have been completed. The same thing can be said about some other family members, including Nancy Rasco and Lyman and Betty Magee, who have provided important support at just the right time in regard to this project.

Finally, a man is nothing without good friends. Therefore, I am forever grateful to some who make my life on a Tennessee mountain more enjoyable day in and day out. These